"Dr. Strasburger writes with rare compassion and passion about the toughest job in the world: to be parents of adolescents in an age when most of the stories about life are told by television. *Getting Your Kids to Say No . . .* is the best guide to making that job more rewarding."

—GEORGE GERBNER, PROFESSOR OF COMMUNICATION AND DEAN EMERITUS OF THE ANNENBERG SCHOOL FOR COMMUNICATION, UNIVERSITY OF PENNSYLVANIA

"This superbly written book by a leader in the field of Adolescent Medicine is a timely primer for parents, physicians and others concerned with the parenting of children and adolescents."

—HYMAN C. TOLMAS, M.D., CLINICAL PROFESSOR OF PEDIATRICS EMERITUS, TULANE UNIVERSITY SCHOOL OF MEDICINE

"Today's complex world and the challenges presented to adolescents can be frightening and confusing. Teens' best helpers should be their parents. This book gives parents both facts and approaches to make them the best resources for their teenagers."

—ROBERT T. BROWN, M.D., CHIEF, SECTION OF ADOLESCENT HEALTH AT CHILDREN'S HOSPITAL, COLUMBUS, OHIO, AND PROFESSOR OF CLINICAL PEDIATRICS AT THE OHIO STATE UNIVERSITY'S COLLEGE OF MEDICINE

Getting Your Kids
to Say No
in the 90s
When You Said Yes
in the 60s

❑

VICTOR STRASBURGER, M.D.

A FIRESIDE BOOK
Published by Simon & Schuster
New York London Toronto Sydney Tokyo Singapore

FIRESIDE

Rockefeller Center
1230 Avenue of the Americas
New York, New York 10020

Copyright © 1993 by Victor Strasburger, M.D.

FIRESIDE and colophon are registered trademarks of Simon & Schuster Inc.

Designed by Irving Perkins Assoc.

Manufactured in the United States of America

10 9 8 7 6 5 4

Library of Congress Cataloging-in-Publication Data
Strasburger, Victor C., date.
    Getting your kids to say no in the 90s when you said yes in the 60s / Victor Strasburger.
      p. cm.
    "A Fireside book."
    Includes bibliographical references and index.
    1. Parent and teenager—United States.   2. Adolescent psychology—United States.   I. Title.
HQ799.15.S77   1993
649'.1—dc20   92-38023
                                                 CIP

ISBN 0-671-79796-4

The author gratefully acknowledges permission from the following sources to reprint material in their control:

Excerpt from article by David Elkind, Ph.D., in *Pediatric Nursing*. Reprinted by permission.

Excerpt from "U.S. Reign of Terror Heightens Nation to World's Leader in Killing, Rape, Theft," March 13, 1991. Copyright © 1991 by the Associated Press. Reprinted by permission.

Excerpt from "Fresh Voices" column by Lynn Minton in *Parade* magazine, April 28, 1991. Copyright © 1991 by *Parade*. Reprinted by permission.

Excerpt from column by John K. Rosemond in the *Charlotte Observer*. Reprinted by permission.

Excerpt from article by George Comerci, M.D. in *Adolescent Medicine: State of the Art Reviews*. Reprinted by permission.

Excerpt from interview by Susan M. Barbieri, May 17, 1992, *Orlando Sentinel*. Reprinted by permission.

Excerpt from "The Quack Epidemic," reprinted by permission of *The New Republic*. Copyright © 1988 by the New Republic, Inc.

Excerpt from Dear Abby column, May 15, 1991. Copyright 1991 Universal Press Syndicate. Reprinted by permission. All rights reserved.

continued on page 287

For Alya, Max, Marg, Suzie, and Mom, with love.

And for Jim: Don't wait for the novel!

Acknowledgments

❏

I don't want to sound *too* much like an Academy Award recipient, but . . . I would like to acknowledge my parents, Marjorie C. Strasburger and the late Arthur C. Strasburger, who raised me with love, affection, and wisdom. The members of the Adolescent Counseling Service at Bridgeport Hospital, Bridgeport, Connecticut, deserve my sincere thanks: Jill Sanislo, Alan Leiman, and Donald Cohen were trusted friends and colleagues, whom I miss. I have also been fortunate in having a number of superb mentors: Dr. Michael Rothenberg at the University of Washington School of Medicine, Dr. Robert Masland at Harvard Medical School, and Dr. L. Clark Hansbarger at the University of New Mexico School of Medicine. Several friends and colleagues continue to teach me "the basics": Drs. Robert Brown, Adele Hofmann, Hy Tolmas, William Long, Jr., Donald Greydanus, and George Comerci. Finally, this book would not have been possible without the encouragement and guidance of my agent, Helen Heller, and my editor, Gail Winston. To all of these people, I am extremely grateful.

You'll have to rethink the whole question.
This getting born is not as simple as it seemed. . . .
It is, time shows, more complicated than either I—or
you—ever dreamed.

> —Robert Penn Warren,
> *New and Selected Poems,*
> *1923–1985*

For every complex problem, there's a simple solution, and it's
wrong.

> —H. L. Mencken

One day in retrospect the years of struggle will strike you as
the most beautiful.

> —Sigmund Freud

Contents

Introduction

❑

Like Peter Pan, we modern parents don't want to grow up. We are the "baby boomers" from the 1950s and 1960s, and our parents always treated us like children. They were strict—sometimes too strict, we thought—and seemed inordinately fond of establishing rules about everything, from sex and drugs to table manners and clothing. They didn't like our "attitude," and back then many of us didn't like theirs, either. So we "just said yes" to sex and drugs and rock 'n' roll, and in college some of us protested the Vietnam War and got tear-gassed for our efforts, and we wore our hair long and our jeans tattered. We thought we'd show them a thing or two. We didn't want to have to grow up—there was nothing very appealing about the prospect of adulthood, especially if we were going to turn out to be exactly like our parents.

But wait just a minute: One day we woke up and things had suddenly changed. Now it's 1993, and we're no longer seventeen years old, in college, and footloose and fancy-free. And who's that standing over there, yelling for Mommy and Daddy? It's our kids!

Why grow up? Because we now have children to take care of, that's why. Now that *we're* the parents, we have to figure out how we're going to play that role. We need to think about what our parents did that was good, what they did that wasn't so good, what they did that irritated us so much, and then begin putting some of it (the good parts) into practice ourselves. But we can't afford to lug around all of the excess baggage we're carrying from the sixties. All of a sudden, we find ourselves thinking like our parents—no sex, no drugs—but at the same time we can still remember what we went through as adolescents. So what's it going to be? The liberal sixties or the conservative nineties. "Sex and drugs and rock 'n' roll" or "home alone" by 11 P.M.? "F—k the Establishment" or "Listen to your parents, we know what's best for you?" Or, to put things in a slightly different perspective, how do you get your kids to say no in the nineties when you said yes in the sixties?

Parenting children has never been more difficult than it is now—because of the complexity of modern society and modern families, because of all the risks that children and teenagers are potentially exposed to (sex, drugs, homicide, suicide, AIDS), and especially because of our reluctance to be as authoritative and unyielding as our parents were. But, lest you think you can get away with just a few generic words of wisdom—like "Just be careful out there" (Sergeant Phil Esterhaus's famous line to his officers in *Hill Street Blues*)—think again. No matter what you do, you run the risk of facing a barrage of embarrassing questions from your kids, like "Did *you* ever smoke cigarettes?" "Did *you* ever use marijuana?" "Did *you* have sex before you were married?" Your children are not dumb.

They know you grew up in the fifties and sixties and even seventies, and they know things were different back then. Do you really think they're going to cut you some slack, Jack? Hell no—they're heading straight for your jugular.

This book is intended to give you some shelter.

Modern parenting is much more of an art than a science. I can't teach you how to be an ideal parent, because there's no such animal. There is no one simple answer for what to do in any given situation, nor are all children susceptible to the same approaches. Parents have different personalities, and so do kids. Sometimes the problem is simply that the two sets of personalities are just not matching up well. Parenting is a more complicated business than what some advice books would have you believe. Therefore, this book is not intended to be either a do-it-yourself manual or an advice book that you can run to every time you have an argument with your child. You won't be able to find out what you *should* have said. Instead, I am going to give you some ideas to consider about how you're raising your children and show you some of the pitfalls to watch out for. If you take the time to read through this book, you may find that your philosophy of child rearing begins to change. You will begin to understand some of the problems that kids face today and begin to empathize with them. Just as it has never been more difficult to be a parent than in the 1990s, it also has never been more difficult to be a kid. But once you begin to consider in what ways you want to raise your kids—the same as or differently from the way your parents raised you, you will probably do just fine, and so will your kids.

The next very obvious question is: Why should you listen to me? (After all, we children of the sixties were experts at challenging authority, weren't we?)

For one thing, like you, I am a parent. That doesn't

necessarily make me an expert, but at the very least you can expect that I will both sympathize *and* empathize with you.

I am also a pediatrician and a specialist in adolescent medicine. For the past twelve years I have been listening to teenagers talk about their parents and to parents talk about their teenagers. I have also watched the progress of a generation of babies through toddlerhood and childhood into adolescence and seen how their parents have tried to cope with the inevitable changes. Currently, I am an associate professor at the University of New Mexico School of Medicine in Albuquerque, where I teach medical students, interns, and residents how to take care of children and adolescents. I have also served on several national committees of the American Academy of Pediatrics and the Society for Adolescent Medicine and as a consultant to the National PTA. As an expert on the effects of the media on children and adolescents, I frequently lecture around the country and get to talk with parents, teachers, and other pediatricians. I know the sorts of things that you're worried about (and, believe me, I'm worried about them, too!).

The origins of this book really go back to the years after I completed my pediatric residency training, when I was a member of the clinical faculty at Yale Medical School. At that time, I founded and directed the Adolescent Counseling Service for teenagers and their parents at a community hospital in Connecticut. We were trying to help hundreds of families deal with their adolescents, and hundreds of adolescents deal with their adolescence. We treated upper-class, middle-class, and lower-class kids of all races and religions. Their problems spanned the range of adolescence—from parents complaining about their daughter's choice of boyfriends and teenagers upset about their parents not giving them enough freedom to teen-

agers attempting suicide, abusing drugs, sexually acting
out, or running away from home. Sometimes the problem
was the teenager's, sometimes the parents', but mostly
both sides were at fault, entangled in a hostile dance of
misguided expectations and poor communications. Much
of what we saw and tried to deal with could have been
avoided or prevented early, *during childhood and preadolescence*. In that sense, problems during adolescence are akin
to cancer: Detect them early and they're curable; wait until
they've metastasized and you're dead.

Like most primary-care specialists, I firmly believe that
the easiest way to cure problems is to prevent them from
occurring in the first place. So this book is meant to be
read before your children reach adolescence, or just when
they begin acting out as teenagers, although we will discuss what to do with later problems as well. But I wrote
this book mostly because I think our generation is getting
shortchanged: We were criticized when we were teenagers; now we're being labeled the "me generation," unable
to think about anyone (including our kids) except ourselves. You know and I know, that that's dead wrong. We
were the first generation to think about trying to change
the existing world order, to challenge authority and, in
the case of the Vietnam War, to actually succeed in catalyzing resistance to it. We are thoughtful, sensitive people
who want to raise our kids to be the same way—but we're
caught in a trap: Do we try to parent our kids the way our
parents raised us, in which case we run the risk of feeling
hopelessly old-fashioned and many worse things, or do
we try to adapt to the changing world and become modern parents? My vote is for modern parenting.

Chapter 1

Why Teenagers Do the (Sometimes Stupid) Things They Do: Normal Adolescent Development

❑

THE PHYSICAL SIDE OF ADOLESCENCE

From a biological viewpoint, being a teenager is like trying to emulate the guy on *The Ed Sullivan Show* who could keep a dozen plates spinning at the end of a dozen long wooden poles. Impressive stuff, but he was probably a nervous wreck by the end of his act. Imagine, as an adult, if you had only ten years to suddenly cope with becoming elderly, your entire body was changing virtually overnight, and you had to redo your entire social network. You might not be very pleasant to live with either! Teenagers have only ten years to accomplish some very serious and difficult psychosocial tasks, and at the same time try to cope with the fact that their height is increasing by 25 percent, their weight is doubling, and they are developing pubic hair and acne and the ability to reproduce. As the Beatles used to sing, "You know it ain't easy."

❑

MARK: *Mark is a fifteen-year-old who comes to see me because he is short and wants "growth hormone shots." In fact, he is not only the shortest boy in his class, he is the shortest person in his class! At five feet one inch and 96 pounds, he feel as if puberty has passed him by. He is in the fifth percentile for height and weight for fifteen-year-old boys. If he were just "average," he would be five feet six and a half and 124 pounds, which would be just fine with him. His male classmates tease him, his female classmates don't view him as "date material," and his grades are beginning to slip because all he can think about is what life would be like if he were a foot taller. Although he is an avid basketball and football player, he doesn't stand a chance to make either team. He finds little solace in the fact that his father was a "late developer" as well.*

KATHY: *Kathy is eleven years old and looks nineteen. Her mother brings her to see me because she is afraid that Kathy is "too mature" and will "get herself into a lot of situations that she can't handle," even though she is not allowed to date. Kathy is five feet five inches tall, weighs 120 pounds, and wears a 36C bra. She has been menstruating for six months. She giggles when I ask about her menstrual periods and looks to her mother to answer for her. She says boys are "a pain" and shows no interest in dating, but her mother says that she is suddenly very popular with all the boys in the eighth and ninth grades. In fact, Kathy reports that her best friend's brother "has the hots" for her and thinks she's "a real babe," this according to her best friend (who has not yet begun menstruating). She is embarrassed to be telling me such things and obviously takes no pleasure in her mature physical appearance.*

❑

Trying to cope with adolescence can be extraordinarily taxing when you feel that your own biology is working against you. Teenagers can be as savvy as political cartoonists in their ability to caricature their peers' most dramatic features, and they hammer away at these sore spots. So Mark becomes "a runt," and Kathy is "stacked."

There are several extremely important principles of growth and development at work here. The first is that there is great *variability* among adolescents in their physical maturation: girls' breasts can begin budding as early as age eight or as late as age thirteen and still be considered normal. Generally, girls will begin menstruating about two to two and a half years after breast buds first appear, and their maximum growth spurt will occur in the six to twelve months before menstruation begins. So when a fourteen-year-old comes to my office and wants to know how much taller she's going to get, and she has been menstruating for a year, I can tell her that she has pretty much reached her adult height, give or take an inch or two. On the average, boys begin developing two years later than girls—just go observe a sixth-grade dance—and the first sign of male puberty is enlargement of the testes, followed by the appearance of pubic hair. This can occur anytime between ages ten and fifteen and still be considered normal.

Yet think about a fully developed eleven-year-old girl like Kathy, most of whose peers will not begin menstruating until age twelve or thirteen. She has the mind of a child, trapped inside an adult woman's body, and she is receiving a great deal of unsolicited and undesired attention from boys, who tend to equate breast development with attractiveness. Many studies show that, fortunately, teenagers behave according to their chronological age, not their physical age, so Kathy's lack of interest in boys is normal and somewhat protective. Not that her mother's concerns aren't appropriate—they are. Kathy has all sorts of feelings about being a "freak of nature" that she may carry into her adult life and that may determine her self-image unless we deal with them now.

Mark, the late developer, is paying the same heavy price for not being "normal," even though he is. Everyone else in his class is beginning to look "adult" and he's still a "shrimp." Girls ignore him. He can't compete athletically against other fourteen- and fifteen-year-olds, who have far more strength and endurance, thanks to their newfound supply of testosterone. His parents try to console him by telling him that he will catch up—which he will—but he feels as if the train has already left the station without him on board. Fortunately, injections of small amounts of testosterone, under the care of a pediatric endocrinologist, will speed his pubertal development without any appreciable risks. Kathy, on the other hand, is stuck with being an early developer.

One suffers because she sticks out in all the wrong places, and the other suffers mostly from insufficient brawn. In our society—male-dominated, macho, and obsessed with female anatomy, especially breasts—the normal physical changes of puberty take on a far greater significance to teenagers than perhaps they deserve. Both of these patients represent teenagers with very common predicaments. To paraphrase Jim (The Doors) Morrison's autobiography: No one gets out of puberty unscathed.

The other important message here is that, as a parent, you can breathe a sigh of relief if your teenager is developing and growing normally—but even pubertal development that is completely normal can have significant psychological consequences. This was confirmed by a very clever research program called the Oakland Growth Study. It found what most high school and middle school teachers already know—that early-maturing males have a distinct advantage over late developers. The researchers selected a group of early and late maturers and followed them from puberty through their thirties, periodically giving them psychological tests and interviewing their teachers, friends, peers, and employers. Early maturers were more poised, relaxed, good-natured, popular, and self-confident. They were the school leaders and the student athletes. As adults, they were people whose advice was frequently sought, who made a good impression and were considered warm and sociable. Late maturers were found to be more restless, impulsive, and self-indulgent; they were more likely to have feelings of inadequacy and rejection, and they used more childish social techniques. In other words, the James Dean type versus the Tom Hanks type. The researchers concluded that pubertal development was the *single best predictor of adult male social success.* Pretty scary stuff (unless, of course, you're male and an early developer).

For girls, the consequences of early versus late maturation are less clear. The Oakland Growth Study found that the exact reverse held for girls: The early maturers suffered from less popularity, prestige, poise, and leadership compared with the late maturers. But other studies have disputed that finding. In one, of 731 girls in the sixth through ninth grades in a suburban California community, one development group seemed to have "most favored status" in each grade. In sixth grade, when the average girl was prepubertal, the late maturers were favored. By ninth grade, the early maturers fared better. In general, there are fewer studies of girls than of boys. As female athleticism becomes better appreciated in our society, the statistics for girls may begin to parallel those for boys.

Another key feature of adolescents' physical development is **disproportion.** Arms, legs, noses, breasts, and chins seem to sprout up with no regard for overall body size. I frequently see teenage girls who are concerned that their breasts are unequal in size, and teenage boys may notice that one testicle is slightly bigger than the other. Nearly everyone has at least a subtle asymmetry, and adults can casually dismiss much of this. But to the average teenager each physical imperfection is magnified a hundred times.

Just when you thought it was safe to come out of the locker room . . . more bad news about puberty. Over half of all fourteen-year-old boys develop some degree of **gynecomastia**—in plain terms, breasts.

❑

JIM: Jim, fourteen, comes to see me because he has been having chest pains for several months. The pains are vague and not well localized, but they do bother him a great deal. He says that he is not worried about whether he's having a heart attack (a very common worry of children and teenagers who have chest pains but don't know that heart attacks are incredibly rare at their age). When he removes his shirt and I examine his chest, I comment that he has "a little extra tissue" beneath his nipple. He tenses immediately. I tell him that having such tissue is extremely common for a fourteen-year-old boy; it doesn't mean that Mother Nature has sent him a special delivery of the wrong hormones or that he is really in the process of developing into a girl. I also inform him that in all likelihood the tissue will disappear in a year or so. He relaxes visibly. On follow-up two months later, his chest pains have disappeared.

❑

In talking to Jim I was extremely careful not to use the word "breasts." Can you imagine struggling with your identity and concept of sexuality and suddenly developing one of the hallmark characteristics of the opposite sex? The amount of tissue is usually minimal (a half inch or an inch in diameter, directly under the nipple), but the degree of development can vary widely. Numerous studies have tried to find a hormonal defect to explain why gynecomastia occurs, but so far none has been found. In more than 90 percent of boys the tissue goes away within three years, but I have sent some male patients for surgical removal of their breast tissue when either the breast development was significant (female-type breasts) or their psychological reaction to it was too extreme.

The physical side of adolescence may be beginning to sound like a conspiracy to torture teenagers. You wouldn't get much disagreement from them. Adolescence is the second-most-rapid period of growth, after infancy. But infants seem to have a lot more fun doing their growing than teenagers do. Nevertheless, parents who are attuned to these sorts of problems and physicians who are used to dealing with adolescents can help at least to minimize the negative effects.

THE COGNITIVE SIDE OF ADOLESCENCE

I know this may not come as news to most of you, but *teenagers do not always think like adults,* even though they *look* exactly like adults. This can get very confusing for parents, other adults, and teenagers themselves. Teenagers look like adults, want to be like adults, but often act and think like children.

The Swiss psychologist Jean Piaget described the development stages of intellectual thought. Teenagers proceed from concrete thinking to being capable of intellectual abstractions ("what if" thinking) by about age sixteen. What this means is that if you say to a twelve-year-old, "I know the sky is blue and the grass is green, but what if the sky were green and the grass blue?" he would say "Don't be silly. That's impossible." But if you asked a sixteen-year-old, she might respond, "Then the moon would shine during the day and the sun at night." Older teenagers are capable of abstract thought. This is an extremely important feature of adolescence, because it determines the success or failure of many health-related interventions aimed at teenagers—for instance, drug-use or pregnancy-prevention programs. As we will see in the following chapters, when such programs are established by adults who expect teenagers to think as they do, the programs inevitably fail. When normal adolescent psychology is taken into account, they have a chance of success.

Having said this, I have to mention several other major shortcomings in adolescent thinking. Piaget noted that 20 to 30 percent of adults *never* acquire the ability to reason abstractly. And even having such an ability does not necessarily enable a person to act intelligently. Some teenagers may still suffer from what Tufts psychologist David Elkind* calls "pseudostupidity": "The capacity to conceive many different alternatives is not immediately cou-

---

* Much of the following discussion comes from the work of Dr. Elkind. He is one of the most thoughtful philosophers about adolescence writing today, and his books (listed in appendix I) are highly recommended.

pled with the ability to assign priorities and to decide which choice is more or less appropriate than others." In other words, although they look like adults, teenagers can think like children, adolescents, or adults. In that sense, dealing with teenagers can sometimes be like having to deal with someone who has a multiple personality, as in *The Three Faces of Eve.* At any one time, you don't know if you're talking to the child, the adolescent, or the adult.

Adolescents' thinking can also be extremely egocentric, as illustrated by the young girl who falls in love for the first time and is exasperated by her mother's questions: "Oh, Mother, you just don't know how it feels to be in love!" The girl cannot discern that what is new in her experience may not be new in the history of Western civilization. Most teenagers are disciples of Ptolemy: The sun and stars revolve around them. This can work to their distinct disadvantage. For example, the teenager with a big nose will naturally assume that everyone thinks he has a big nose. It's pointless trying to argue with him, even if you know that his nose is not all that big.

In addition to their egocentrism, many teens share a common fantasy—the *foundling fantasy*—in which they imagine that they are not the offspring of their actual parents but of much wiser and more attractive people who were forced to give them up in infancy for adoption. During the 1970s, for example, a majority of teenagers surveyed by one national women's magazine reported that they would gladly trade their parents for Mary Tyler Moore and Robert Redford. Today it would be Paula Abdul and Michael Jordan.

Sometimes adolescents create an *imaginary audience* for themselves, as if they were always onstage, being scrutinized by others whose sole mission in life is to observe and comment on their clothes or complexion. Teenagers begin to believe that everyone else is always thinking about what they are thinking about—them! This belief can explain a lot of adolescent behavior. For example, the need to play to the imaginary audience helps to explain the extreme self-consciousness of adolescents. But at the same time, teens *want* to be looked at and thought about, because that confirms their sense of self-worth.

A belief in the imaginary audience also has important implications for adolescents with various illnesses. For example, parents are sometimes amazed at how well their handicapped child can do with a significant disability (such as an amputation, diabetes, a kidney disease requiring dialysis) but then are surprised when the child's ability to cope suddenly deteriorates during early adolescence. Why? Because only then are the youngsters beginning to look at themselves the way others see them. Likewise, teenagers are notoriously reluctant to see psychiatrists or psychologists for fear that the imaginary audience will view them as "mental cases." Many of the teenagers I have seen who have made suicide attempts have had very rich fantasies about how their death would play to the imaginary audience: "They'll be sorry they treated me like that . . . Everyone will be crying at my funeral," etc. Similarly, adolescents who engage in acts of vandalism—which seem so senseless and irrational to us—actually may be destroying property because they can imagine the audience's reaction (how the school principal will feel and react).

The imaginary audience may also contribute to the onset of eating disorders in adolescents, such as anorexia nervosa or obesity, according to Elkind. Affected teenagers are not worried about the imaginary audience's opinion of their bodies; rather, they want the audience to believe that they have their eating under control. In an article in *Pediatric Nursing* (November–December 1984) he describes how they try to hide their eating from others:

Obese adolescents, like obese adults, try to give the impression—in public eating places—that they have no appetite. They pick at their food and use artificial sweeteners, giving the impression to the audience of what I have called "immaculate obesity." Such individuals try to insinuate that they become fat through breathing the air, and not because they overindulge in food. That is why they seem relatively unconcerned with how they look. They have displaced their concern from what the audience thinks about their bodies to what the audience thinks about their impulse control.

With anorexia nervosa, too, teenagers actually are concerned about demonstrating to the audience that they have control over their impulses: that they were blessed with a thin body and the capacity to eat without becoming overweight—"divine thinness." Therefore, with both groups of affected teenagers, appeals that focus on their appearance may be unsuccessful. Approaches that deal with their impulse control and other issues of control will likely be more successful.

❑

MARISSA. Marissa is a fourteen-year-old straight-A student whom I took care of one summer that I spent as a camp doctor. She had been losing weight for six months. Initially, she and her mother had decided to diet together. When Marissa lost twenty pounds and wanted to continue dieting, her mother became concerned. Marissa also began exercising intensively and insisting on choosing the evening menu for the family, despite not wanting to eat dinner herself. Her menstrual periods, which had been normal, ceased. At parents' visiting day, her mother tried to convince her that at 91 pounds and five feet four inches she was much too thin and becoming unattractive.

Marissa strongly disagreed. Her mother stood her in front of a mirror and suggested that she looked like a concentration camp victim. Marissa said that she wanted to "just lose five more pounds here" (pointing to her already slim hips). Her parents and I decided that to stay at camp, Marissa would have to gain one pound per week toward her ideal weight of 105 pounds. After two weeks, Marissa weighed 88 pounds and was sent home, to be hospitalized in an adolescent medical unit that specialized in treating patients with anorexia nervosa. After several weeks of inpatient treatment, and several months of individual and family therapy, her weight stabilized at 102 pounds.

❑

Of course, the imaginary audience is not unique to adolescents. We all sometimes slip back to our early adolescence and have fantasies of acting opposite Meryl Streep or Robert De Niro in a movie, or playing a singles match on Centre Court in Wimbledon, or appearing at Carnegie Hall or on Broadway. And we've all had the experience of walking into a crowded room and hearing laughter and thinking that we were the subject of the conversation. These are temporary lapses, at most. But much of what motivates the behavior of early adolescents is contained in this concept.

Similarly, teenagers often seen themselves as actors in their own *personal fable*. Their lives take on heroic proportions. As the Girl in *The Fantasticks* sings: "I am special. *I am special*. Please, God, *please*: Don't let me be normal." This represents a kind of Superman/Supergirl complex, which adults find particularly annoying—teenagers think they are invulnerable.

Again this sort of concept helps to explain much adolescent behavior. A sixteen-year-old is perfectly capable of counseling her best friend to use birth control, should she have intercourse, but then not using it herself—pregnancy "can't happen to me." Why do teenagers experiment with alcohol and then, worse yet, get behind the wheel of a car? Surely they know better, and intellectually they certainly do. But their personal fable tells them that they are special and therefore not subject to the ordinary laws of nature that apply to everyone else. Similarly, teenagers with chronic illnesses may believe that they do not have to take their medicines or comply with prescribed therapy. Why? Because, in deference to the imaginary audience, they do not want to appear different; but at the same time, their personal fable tells them that they *are* different and can cope quite well without treatment (although others with the same disease should of course comply with therapy). Adolescent risk-taking behavior appears less risky if teens believe that they are invulnerable. This sort of behavior infuriates adults, who think that teenagers are simply acting irresponsibly. But the real issue is cognitive processing and intellectual maturation, *not* willfulness.

In *The Growth of Logical Thinking* (Basic Books, 1958), Piaget described the personal fables of one class of high school seniors in a small Swiss town:

> One of them, who has since become a shopkeeper, astonished his friends with his literary doctrines and wrote a novel in secret. Another, who has since become the director of an insurance company, was interested, among other things, in the future of the theater and showed some close friends the first scene of the first act of a tragedy—and then got no further. A third, taken up with philosophy, dedicated himself to no less a task than the reconciliation of science and religion. We do not even have to enumerate the social and political reformers found on both right and

left. There were only two members of the class who did not reveal any astounding life plans. Both were more or less crushed under strong "superegos" of parental origin, and we do not know what their secret daydreams might have been.

Fortunately, belief in one's personal fable tends to diminish with age. Once teenagers develop close relationships with friends, they quickly discover that they are not quite as unique as they once thought (and not as lonely, either). But a vestige of the personal fable remains with us as adults. It helps to soften the impact of aging, and in particular the mid-life crisis, when adults begin to wonder exactly what they have accomplished during their first thirty-five or forty years. Adults can see some of their friends stricken with cancer or heart disease, or themselves be faced with a strong family history of a particular disease, but still be capable of thinking. "It can't happen to me." In such cases the personal fable represents adaptive behavior and is better known by its alternative name: denial.

Teenagers' apparent hypocritical behavior is also related to the personal fable. Adolescents resemble two-year-olds in this regard. You can't expect two-year-olds to say "please" and "thank you" appropriately, even if you constantly remind them to, because they lack the ability to understand the linkage between the two concepts. Similarly, teenagers' ability to understand certain general principles of behavior is not necessarily linked to their ability to put principle into practice. One of my favorite cartoons shows a set of bewildered parents looking at their teenager's room, which looks as if a cyclone has recently struck. One says to the other: "He doesn't have time to straighten it up. He's out picketing for a cleaner environment." Again, as with the personal fable, the rules don't apply to the particular teenager. It helps if you view this as a problem of intellectual or cognitive immaturity, not a fatal defect in moral character.

One aspect of adolescence that we tend to lose as adults is *idealism*, and it's the one cognitive trait that we, as baby boom parents, should most readily identify with, since most of us possessed abundant quantities of it. In literature it's called *Weltschmerz* (world pain), as exemplified by characters like Huck Finn, Anne Frank, and Holden Caulfield. When teenagers complain that no one understands them, they are usually referring to this side of themselves: the idealistic, caring young person, searching for an ideal and decent world for his ideal and decent self to inhabit. "Never trust anyone over thirty" may actually mean don't trust anyone who understands how hard it is to actually realize your ideals. This, in fact, may represent the origin of the "generation gap," according to Elkind—the conflict between adolescent idealism and adult pragmatism. Granted, a large part of idealism may actually be a resistance to growing up. But how many of us adults have lost all of our change-the-world fervor? Just look at pictures of the Chicago Seven in the 1960s and now. The radicals of the sixties have become the establishment of the nineties, with precious few exceptions. Wouldn't the world be a better place if adults were able to retain some of their adolescent idealism?

Understanding the cognitive side of adolescence can give parents a new perspective on the seemingly irrational behavior their teenagers exhibit. Yes, they are intellectually immature; but isn't that to be expected? In a society as complex as ours, one wouldn't expect children to immediately be able to function emotionally and intellectually as adults simply because they have achieved physical adulthood. As Elkind sums up:

Piaget, then, has helped us to shift a whole new set of behaviors from the realm of the "bad" to the realm of "behavior typical for this age group." This is not to say that because these behaviors are "normal" we should ignore or neglect them. What I suggest is that we understand why adolescents sometimes act "dumb," boorish, insensitive or hypocritical; that we deal with it calmly and without a sense of moral outrage. If we recognize that these behaviors reflect intellectual immaturity, we can ourselves be more rational in our reactions to young people.

THE PSYCHOLOGICAL SIDE OF ADOLESCENCE

It's not easy growing up—never has been, never will be. In fact, from the earliest recorded history, critics have taken potshots at adolescents and their behavior:

The Greek historian Hesiod (eighth century B.C.): "I see no hope for the future of our people if they are dependent on the frivolous youth of today, for certainly all youth are reckless beyond words. . . . When I was a boy, we were taught to be discreet and respectful of elders, but the present youth are exceedingly wise and impatient of restraint."

Aristotle: "The young are in character prone to desire and ready to carry any desire they may have formed into action. Of bodily desires it is the sexual in which they are most disposed to give way, and in regard to sexual desire they exercise no self-restraint."

Shakespeare: "I wish there were no age between ten and three-and twenty, or that youth would sleep out the rest, for there is nothing in the between but getting wenches with child, wronging the ancientry, fighting. . . ."

Mark Twain: "When I was fourteen I was amazed at how ignorant my father was, but when I reached the age of twenty-one I was surprised how much he had learned in seven years." Also: "There is a charm about the forbidden that makes it unspeakably desirable."

George Bernard Shaw: "Youth is wasted on the young."

What are all of these keen observers of human nature trying to tell us? First, adolescence has always been a difficult time for children to negotiate their way through, and adults have never stopped complaining about them as they do it. Modern parents' notion that "today's kids are just plain rotten" is a theme song that has been played over and over since the earliest recorded history. Second, it is the sexual nature of adolescents that adults most object to. Drugs and alcohol would probably place a close second. (In ancient Egypt, hieroglyphics accused teenagers of being good for little else but drinking too much beer and passing out in the garden.) Third, a certain amount of antiestablishment hostility can be expected from many adolescents. And fourth, we are primarily talking (and complaining) about *Western* adolescents.

Historical Adolescence

Although adults have complained about young people from the earliest recorded history, adolescence as we know it is a recent phenomenon. The ancient Greeks did believe in a transition from childhood to adulthood: Plato thought that the primary task of youth was to develop rational thinking; Aristotle thought that it was learning to make choices. This philosophy persisted until the Renaissance, when the discovery of sperm cells (each thought to contain a fully formed human being, or homunculus) meant that children were really nothing more than miniature adults. Maturity was equated with independence.

In colonial America, children often were apprenticed away from home as soon as they were able to work. They were expected to contribute to the family's support. Although economically dependent on their masters, they were completely free of parental guidance. The Industrial Revolution prompted nineteenth-century school reforms, since workers required more training to handle the new machines. Meanwhile, Locke's theory of the mind as a blank slate (tabula rasa) meant that children required moral guidance as well as experience, and Rousseau revived the notion that youth require a period of time for nurturance and protection. Children were no longer miniature adults, and parents assumed increased responsibility for raising them properly.

In America these economic and philosophic trends merged in the early 1900s, when a modern concept of adolescence began to emerge. Compulsory education to age sixteen, child labor legislation, and a juvenile justice system all served to redefine the boundaries between childhood, adolescence, and adulthood and to emphasize the special nature of adolescence. However, in the late twentieth century American adolescents are beginning to again experience the kind of semi-independence that colonial adolescents had, but for different reasons. The parental prerogative has once again been influenced by economic factors. With more than 50 percent of women now working, more families have both parents at work rather than at home. Add to this the U.S. divorce rate— the highest in the Western world—and the equation indicates that adolescents are increasingly free of parental guidance and constraints. With increasing leisure time and increased purchasing power, adolescents enjoy a new kind of relationship with adults, whom they see primarily in controlled environments (such as school or church) or on television. Friends, peers, and the media play more significant roles than ever before. Economic factors also make it imperative to keep adolescents out of the work force as long as possible, to reduce adult unemployment. This, combined with higher education, may prolong modern adolescence into the third decade of life.

Cultural Adolescence

Adolescence can also be viewed as a cultural phenomenon, not a cruel trick of Mother Nature or a communist plot. Although the physical changes of adolescence are significant, and may have lifelong repercussions, adolescents' behavior cannot be blamed on their hormones alone. Contrary to the popular media, teenagers are not "hormones with legs" or "hormones in search of trouble." In many cultures teenagers undergo none of the behavior that we take to be characteristic of them. But these are non-Western societies, in which children become adults through a relatively simple and straightforward "rite of passage."

Rites of passage are characterized by three elements: separation, transition, and reincorporation. Adolescents who are approaching physical maturity are separated from their families and taken to an initiation hut or a mountain site, where they undergo a short period of seclusion, instruction, testing, and other rituals, following which they are reincorporated back into the community as adults. For boys, the ritual may be traumatic (for example, circumcision with a sharpened stick among the Aborigines, or having an incisor knocked out among the Yuin and Murring tribes in Australia), or it may be relatively simple (wearing a red loincloth and going to live among the men for Truk natives). For girls, initiation into womanhood usually coincides with menarche (first menstrual period) and often involves seclusion, and the rituals may encompass such practices as clitoridectomy.

Margaret Mead did much of the landmark work in this area in Samoa in the early 1900s (*Coming of Age in Samoa* was published in 1928). She described the transition to adolescence in Samoa as very peaceful and easy, because the entire community had similar values and family ties did not have to be broken. Among those values was their view of sex as a pleasurable and natural activity, both in and out of marriage. In Samoa, rites of passage were not even needed.

Other anthropologists have studied initiation rites in non-Western societies in great detail. Among Kikuyu boys in Kenya, fifteen-year-olds are circumcised, adopted by ritual parents, and smeared with earth in an eight-day ceremony of dancing, singing, and learning warrior arts, after which they rejoin the tribe as warriors. In Surinam, along the Maroni River, Carib girls are confined to a house once they begin menstruating so that the river and forest spirits will not be offended by the bleeding. Dressed in old clothes, they eat special foods and are bathed by a trusted elderly couple. They are given a tuft of burning cotton to hold, which they shift from hand to hand rapidly, to symbolize that they should always be industrious and keep their hands busy. They must place their hands in a bowl of stinging ants, to symbolize that they will work as hard as ants do. Finally, dressed in special clothing and wearing special jewelry, they are led back to a celebration ceremony in the village.

Regardless of what puberty rite is practiced, it is a single, simple (albeit sometimes painful) indoctrination into adult society, and adult status is easily achieved—virtually overnight. Even the most elaborate rites last only a few weeks. In a sense, these societies have bypassed adolescence, or at least shortened it to a week at most. Consequently, they have no problem with rebellious, sullen, acting-out teenagers, because such people simply don't exist. The new initiates are welcomed back into the tribe as adults, having "paid their dues" quickly and in a manner that is clear-cut and known about ahead of time.

I have met many parents who would gladly sign their kids up for such rites if they existed in the United States, but, of course, we have a more complicated society. In other societies in which everyone holds similar views and values, identity is easy to achieve. How difficult is it to accept particular values and roles when they are the only ones that a young person ever sees or knows about? But contemporary Western societies are characterized by conflicting values, and modern technology and transportation guarantee that children and adolescents will be exposed to a variety of opinions on everything from love and sex and marriage to religion, politics, and morality. So Western teenagers experience no single rite of passage.

But they do undergo a series of incomplete—and, for them, often frustrating—*"rites of passage."* Cynical adults might prefer to call such rites as "playing-acting at being an adult." For instance, Jewish males undergoing a bar mitzvah at age thirteen traditionally used to intone, "Today I am a man." Of course, in contemporary American society that is simply a ludicrous notion, except perhaps physically. Thirteen-year-olds can't drink, vote, or legally consume alcohol. Many have barely completed half of their education. They have virtually no adult status, and American society will not be particularly interested in them for another five to ten years, when they can join the armed forces or begin to compete for adult jobs. If the bar mitzvah were not fixed by tradition at age thirteen, it might be better placed at age twenty-one, or even twenty-five, for such a statement to hold true today.

Obtaining a driver's license has always been an important milestone for adolescents, but at age sixteen they still
must rely on the kindness of their parents to pay for the
insurance and provide access to the family car. Voting at
age eighteen is often no big deal for today's politically
apathetic teenagers. Age twenty-one tends to be more significant—both for legalized drinking and for feeling
"adult." But many twenty-one-year-olds are still dependent on their parents financially, and they may remain so
well into their twenties and thirties if they go on to graduate school.

There are also many less formal incomplete rites of passage: sleeping over at a friend's house, going to overnight
summer camp, being allowed to take public transportation
alone, arranging one's own social schedule. None of
them, individually, amounts to much in terms of adult
status, but each helps in its own little way at least to as-
sure a child or teenager that she is getting there. (Of
course, according to every child, each such privilege is
granted *years* after everyone else was allowed to do it.)

So when does a teenager in the United States become
an adult? Much of what angers us as adults is that adolescents frequently "play at" becoming adults, or gradually
attain adulthood through the "two steps forward, one
step back" approach. Instead of rites of passage, teenagers
think that they have *"rights* of passage"—generally, several years before we think they are ready. But, of course,
given a society in which there is no single, clear path to
adulthood, or even a good standard of when one achieves
adulthood, such imperfect attempts are to be expected.

We adults are ambivalent about our children's growing
up. Many would agree with Shaw that "youth is wasted
on the young." By the time we reach forty or fifty, we can
appreciate much more what life is all about, yet we no
longer have the youthful energy and physique that we did

as a teenager. Much of our culture is youth-oriented, and what first becomes popular among teenagers (fashions, music videos) eventually percolates through adult society as well. In fact, adolescents could be considered as constituting their own subculture within adult society, with an appreciable influence of its own. When many of us began protesting the Vietnam War, we "changed the world." Perhaps as adults we need to recognize and appreciate the next generation's desire and ability to be agents of change. After all, we are the ones whose parents encouraged us to be better than they and to rebel against the "old world" traditions.

UNIVERSAL CHARACTERISTIC OF WESTERN ADOLESCENCE

As we've already discussed, dealing with a teenager sometimes can be like trying to talk with someone who has a multiple-personality disorder: You're never quite sure which person you're trying to address, or who will answer back—the child, the adolescent, or the young adult. But adolescents are just as ambivalent about becoming adults as adults are about letting them grow up. On the one hand, teenagers want all of the rights and privileges of being grown up (such as the freedom to come and go as they please) without any of the responsibilities that go hand-in-hand with those rights (letting people who worry about you know where you are and how you can be reached). From a parent's point of view, this is one of the single most annoying characteristics of teenagers. At the stroke of midnight on his sixteenth birthday, your son wants the car keys deposited in his outstretched palm. Worrying about who is going to pay the extra thousand dollars for car insurance is *your* problem, not his. Yet, if you understand normal adolescent psychology, you can anticipate such behavior (although certainly that does not mean that it must be condoned).

In all fairness to today's teenagers, we must acknowledge several important points. Most importantly, not all teenagers are inherently rebellious or angry or acting out. Some new research seems to indicate that about 80 percent of teenagers cope with adolescence relatively smoothly, and the really difficult teen with severe social or emotional problems is unusual. The kind of behavior that we are primarily discussing here is the more ordinary, day-to-day, bothersome type, rather than anything pathological.

Another important point to remember is that teenagers may look as if they're age nineteen and act as if they're age twelve, but *it's not their fault*, especially if they *are* actually twelve. The average age of menarche in the United States is now twelve and a half years. That means that approximately half of all thirteen-year-olds are biologically capable of having babies. No one in her right mind thinks that this is a very good idea. Yet we have no choice in the matter; it's a fact of life. Early-maturing young girls, in particular, can be very alarming to parents, who are well aware of the premium American society places on female sexuality and consequently the risks involved (rape, sexism, etc.). What's important to understand is that adolescents have not always developed this early and it is *not* their fault (or for that matter, their choice). In the nineteenth century the average age of menarche was sixteen, and this remains the case in some underdeveloped countries. Western society has industrialized the economy and improved nutrition and health care to such a degree that teenagers' biological clocks have become maximally accelerated. To rail against the fact that "kids today are developing too damn fast" or to subconsciously blame kids for their own rapid development is not only unfair but hypocritical—because *we* are directly responsible for producing the environment that makes puberty possible at age ten or twelve. Fortunately, it does not seem biologically likely that kids will develop any more quickly than now.

We sometimes overlook the fact that we ask teenagers to do an incredible number of tasks in a very short time (and one could add that we give them precious little help as well). From age twelve to twenty-one—nine short years —children have to experience all of the physical vicissitudes of adolescence while accomplishing all of the following in order to become "successful adults":

- Establish a strong sense of identity, self-esteem, and self-worth
- Develop a sense of self-sufficiency and independence, both financial and emotional, from their parents
- Establish good relationships with their peers
- Begin to establish successful relationships with the opposite sex and learn to appreciate the difference between love and lust, intimacy and sex
- Decide on career goals and begin training to achieve them

These are serious and difficult psychosocial tasks, and many adults have not yet accomplished them completely. And they require a good deal of time and energy—hence teenagers' remarkable ability to be both incredibly *idealistic* and incredibly *narcissistic* simultaneously. Because of the time pressures that adolescents face, it is inevitable that they spend a good deal of time looking inward—in other words, being egocentric or narcissistic. Parents often complain that their teenagers are obsessed with their own appearance, thoughts, and well-being, to the complete exclusion of everything and everyone else. They can see only their own point of view, which may be extremely narrow. And often it is the combination of idealism and narcissism in such close proximity that is confusing to parents (and to teenagers as well).

Adolescents also have a genuine *ambivalence about growing up*. Remember the song from *Peter Pan*—"I Won't Grow Up"? That could well serve as the subconscious national anthem for many teenagers. On the one hand, there are many advantages to being a child. Your needs are taken care of. You don't have to earn your own living. If you need some money, hey—ask Mom or Dad. You don't even have to plan your own schedule. You don't have any of those weighty responsibilities, like taxes and earning a living, that to some adults are like yokes.

On the other hand, being a child also means that you have none of the privileges of being an adult—and there are many: freedom to do what you want, when you want, without having to get someone's permission; freedom to drink and smoke and have sex; freedom to spend money the way you see fit; freedom to talk and dress and act the way you want to, without being held accountable by your parents. There's a lot to be said for being an adult! Just remember when you went off to college and suddenly your time was completely your own. If you wanted to stay up all night with your friends, you could. If you wanted to watch soap operas all afternoon, you could. Suddenly, *anything* was possible.

The catch here is that teenagers want all of the *privileges* of being an adult without any of the *responsibilities* that go with them. Parents view the ability to handle responsibility as a mark of maturity, whereas teenagers see responsibilities as being imposed on them by adults and therefore degrading tokens of their inferior status.

One inevitable byproduct of all of this turmoil surrounding identity and self-discovery is an almost maniacal *need for privacy.* If you've got a very short time to accomplish something, such as developing a sense of identity, you need to be left alone so that you can fantasize, try on and perfect various social "masks," or talk on the phone for hours to your friends. A parent's respecting this need demonstrates respect for the entire process of a teenager's having a life of his own. Interestingly, the latest teenage jibe at parents has become "Get a life." Perhaps because that is precisely what the teens themselves are most anxious about.

❏

ERIC: Eric is a thirteen-year-old who reluctantly comes to see me with his parents. When asked, he says that he feels fine, doesn't have any problems, doesn't want to talk with me, and doesn't know why he even has to see me. His parents, on the other hand, think that Eric may have a brain tumor. For more than six months he has been sullen and moody, and he now tends to avoid them, whereas previously he was a happy-go-lucky child who was very affectionate toward them. Being intelligent and medically sophisticated, they feel that he has undergone a "complete personality change" and therefore would like him to have a complete neurological exam and a CAT scan.

❏

Eric doesn't have a brain tumor; he does have a condition known as early adolescence! More specifically, whether he is aware of it or not, he is now engaged in behavior that is specifically intended to distance himself from his parents. They are hurt by it but also worried that it may represent some underlying physical disorder. Teenagers have a variety of "tricks" that they can use to help sever ties with their parents and achieve the critical velocity needed to begin establishing their own orbit as young adults.

The "Invisible Parent Syndrome"

Parents are often amazed at how shabbily their teenagers treat them. Almost overnight, their offspring are transformed from loving and affectionate children to standoffish adolescents. Suddenly parents are lepers. Their teenagers are embarrassed to be seen with them in public or even to bring friends home to meet them. We refer to this as the "invisible parent syndrome." Home becomes little more than a hotel, with free room and board, laundry service, and use of the phone. Chores, if they are done at all, are accomplished in a convict-labor fashion. When I talk to parents, what they frequently miss most are the early stages of infancy and early childhood, when they could nuzzle their offspring and feel close to them. They miss being physically close to their teenagers and resent when their teenagers twist and squirm away from any display of physical affection, particularly in public. Teenage sons are particularly embarrassed by maternal affection, and teenage daughters don't quite know how to act with their fathers anymore (and vice versa). The mistake that parents make is to take this sudden physical shyness personally. Your teenager's drive for independence and identity *demands* that she separate from you in this fashion. Fortunately, once these issues have been adequately resolved, toward late adolescence, teenagers are able to reestablish their old bonds of affection.

The " 'Oh Mom/Oh Dad' Syndrome"

If teenagers aren't completely ignoring you, then they're enjoying trying to make you feel like dinosaurs. While you're telling them to grow up, they're telling you how old-fashioned your ideas are and how everyone else is doing it differently. It is actually one of their highest (albeit unintentional) compliments. Of course, as a product of the sixties, you probably never thought that this would ever happen to you. You pictured yourself as being perpetually hip. However, in order to formulate their own ideas and standards, your children first have to question the ones they've grown up with—yours! It's not a pleasant process, but it is a necessary one. Parents should avoid taking this sort of reaction personally or at face value. Complaints and skepticism do not necessarily indicate that values are being rejected—just questioned.

The "Parents Don't Get No Respect Syndrome"

Not only has your placid and loving child turned into an emotional iceberg around you, but he suddenly starts snapping at you, often for no reason at all. Previously you were perfect; now nothing you do is good enough. Yet this sort of skepticism *must* occur. Why? Can you remember back to when you were seven or eight years old? At that age, your parents seemed like giant redwood trees: tall, stately, perfect, permanent. Now you are in your thirties or forties, and your parents are aging rapidly. You may even have to take charge of looking after them. The giant redwood forest is dying. Teenagers *must* begin to see the imperfections in their parents in order to gain the necessary momentum to begin heading for their own separate lives. Otherwise, who would want to break away from utopia and perfection? The result is that the parents' entire generation is questioned and at times even ridiculed. As Anne Frank remarked in her diary: "Why do grown-ups quarrel so easily, so much, and over the most idiotic things. . . . I'm simply amazed again and again over their awful manners and especially their stupidity.''

The All-Important Peer Group

As if having your every decision questioned weren't bad enough, suddenly your child's peer group becomes *the* apparent authority on everything from clothes and music to dating and schoolwork. What you say seems to count for very little. Understandably, parents have a difficult time accepting this. For one thing, it's undeniably true that you know a lot more about everything than the thirteen-year-olds your youngster associates with. For another parents recognize that the peer group can exert a tremendous amount of pressure on their child to engage in such risk-taking behaviors as smoking, drinking beer, and having sex. On the other hand, *there is not just one peer group out there*, composed of sex-crazed, alcohol-swilling teenagers who begin circling your house after dark once your child turns thirteen, waiting for the right moment to lure her into unspeakable acts of adolescent derring-do. There are *many* peer groups to choose from: the jocks, the brains, the socs (sociables), the slackers, the preppies, the "in" group, the "out" group, etc. To a great extent, your teenager's choice of a peer group depends upon his self-image up until that point and therefore is, indirectly, a measure of your parenting success to date. In addition, we've seen how important it is for teenagers to break away from their parents, and the peer group becomes crucial in this process, because it gives teens a new safety net—a new superego figure. Teens then have something to break away *to* and some moral (or immoral, depending on your viewpoint) support for doing it. For early adolescents (ages ten to fourteen) the peer group becomes a kind of mirror; such youngsters are not satisfied with what they think about themselves and require some external validation, which the peer group is happy to provide.

There is no question that the peer group is a major annoyance for parents. But you need to remember that the need for popularity often was learned from you and your spouse. After all, you are just as anxious for your teenager to be popular and well-liked as she is. The only problem is, it's a tough call to say exactly whom you want your teenager to be liked *by*, particularly when the opposite sex is involved. To many parents, almost every adolescent other than their own seems like a potentially evil influence.

Fortunately, the peer group is not all-powerful for the rest of one's life. As identity develops and progresses, teenagers begin to see that at times they can act or think differently from the rest of their peer group and not lose them as friends. In return, they learn to accept behavior in their peers that they know would not be right or appropriate for themselves.

Symbols and Fads

Teenagers adopt certain universal symbols to delineate how much they are different from their parents and other adults: rock music, torn jeans, earrings for males, a different lingo, etc. It is a well-known paradox that when a teenager wants to assert his own individuality, he chooses to do it by conforming to whatever ridiculous fads are prevailing at the time: Mohawk haircuts, ritualistic handshakes, many pierced ear lobes, streaked hair, weird lingo —you name it and it's been tried. These are examples of minor rebellion against adult authority, not wholescale war, yet many adults succumb to the inevitable temptation and try to make an issue out of them. Of course, that is precisely what teenagers want!

At the same time, we baby boom parents need to realize that we have co-opted some of our teenagers' favorite symbols and fads. After all, we were the quintessential rebellious adolescents—the Woodstock generation—and we still take great pride in that fact. Most of us grew up with rock music and still listen to "golden oldies" (which is what we are now in the process of becoming). We still wear jeans and sneakers and outrageous T-shirts. What do our kids do for an encore? Just look at how many television commercials these days use rock 'n' roll music. Unwittingly, we have made "normal adolescent rebellion" more difficult. The fact that we grew up with mainstream rock 'n' roll has pushed our teenagers into heavy metal. I am convinced that if we sat around listening to Aerosmith and the Dead Kennedys all day and watched MTV all night, our kids would probably be forced to return to classical music to maintain their adolescent integrity. Likewise, now that jeans have become a standard item of adult wear, new fashions must be invented to satisfy teenagers' need to be different and to *show off* that difference.

"Up the Establishment"

This particular mark of rebelliousness should be familiar to all of us: a healthy skepticism about how intelligent adults really are and what kind of world they have created. We once felt this way ourselves and went to vocal and sometimes dangerous lengths to express our outrage at the Establishment—Kent State, the Black Panther rallies in New Haven, antiwar protests, draft resistance, etc. Even those who weren't very political or antiwar still demonstrated a healthy skepticism about your parents and other adults: You laughed when they couldn't understand the appeal of the Beatles, and you tried smoking or drinking even though you knew your parents would kill you if they ever found out.

We sometimes forget that teenagers are not dumb. As Groucho Marx once said, "I wouldn't want to become a member of any club that would have me." Teenagers are checking out the "adult club" that they will eventually have to join. But they are also innately suspicious of it.

And why shouldn't they be? Allow me to speak here as an older adolescent might: "Adults have succeeded in screwing up the world, from environmental pollution to the continued threat of war. In the United States we spend more money on weapons of destruction than we do on child health care, more on servicing the national debt than on educating our children. Adults say one thing, like 'just say no' to drugs, and then drink themselves silly. If they get caught for drunken driving, they hire themselves a good lawyer and get off with a slap on the wrist. Then they have a cow if we so much as look at a beer in the refrigerator. Our parents' generation is the first one in United States history in which a President has resigned to avoid impeachment, a movie star has twice been elected as President, we have lost a war (Vietnam) we never should have begun and twenty years later found ourselves in another useless war, the country is threatened with bankruptcy thanks to greedy bankers and an inept Congress, a sizable portion of the American population has become homeless, and on and on . . . Who says we can't do a better job than they have done? Adults want to hold us to impossibly high standards while they themselves do whatever they damn well please, no matter how unethical, illegal, or immoral it may be."

Contrary to many parents' popular belief, your teenagers' goal in life is not to make you miserable. It is to maneuver their way successfully through their adolescence, with a minimum of stress (to them, not to you). But whether you are aware of it or not, you may be part of the problem instead of being part of the solution. Here are the seven most common mistakes that parents make in the "letting go" process, consequently getting caught up in their adolescent's struggles:

1. *Panicking.* If I mention the word "adolescence" to parents of eight- to twelve-year-olds, often their pupils dilate, their breathing becomes labored, and their eyes start to roll back. They are scared to death of the next five to ten years, and their kids already know it. So they try to overcompensate by giving their kids a quick fix of parental guidance ahead of time. All the sex education that should have been accomplished gradually during the past several years is suddenly thrown at the kid, or the parents suddenly want to have long discussions about drugs. This simply doesn't work. Adolescence is a period of *apparent* diminished parental control over children. But, in fact, you've got more control and influence than you probably realize. After all, who parented your children for the ten or twelve years until adolescence? You. Whose values have they been exposed to for their entire lives? Yours. It comes as a shock to many parents that what happens during adolescence has been preordained by what has occurred before, from about age five onward. (See chapters 7 and 8 for a discussion of what to do during these years to avoid difficulties during adolescence.) In a sense, whether your child has a difficult adolescence or not is a test of your parenting skills up to that point. In addition, remember that 80 percent of all children make it through their adolescence with little if any difficulty.

2. *Reluctance to Let Go.* Letting go can be a very difficult and agonizing process, no doubt about it. After all, you know your child's weaknesses better than anyone else, and you have spent the past twelve years playing the Great Protector (and appropriately so). In addition, you know how perilous the outside world can be and how unprepared your kids are to make their way in it, especially these days. Here is the lead story from many newspapers across the country on March 13, 1991:

U.S. Reign of Terror Heightens
Nation to World's Leader in Killing, Rape, Theft

WASHINGTON—The United States is "the most violent and self-destructive nation on Earth," the Senate Judiciary Committee said in a report released yesterday. . . .

The nation's citizens committed a record number of killings in 1990—at least 23,300, or nearly three an hour—and a record number of rapes, robberies and assaults, the committee said. . . .

The report noted that the murder rate in the United States was more than twice that of Northern Ireland, which is torn by civil war; four times that of Italy; nine times England's and 11 times Japan's. . . .

It is scary to think of your child being on her own in such a society. And parents of daughters probably have the most to worry about, given the pervasiveness of crimes against women. Although it may sound overly simplistic, the best defense is a good offense: raising children to be self-reliant, capable of thinking on their own, resourceful. Children with inner strengths are far more resistant to stress and to peer pressure.

There are also times when it seems as if your cute little baby has turned into a young Frankenstein monster virtually overnight, and you'd be delighted if he went to live with one of his aunts or uncles for the next ten years. One of the key lessons for parents is to learn how and when to let go—which is what most of the second half of this book will be about—not whether or not to let go. Parents often feel that they would gladly sacrifice themselves for their children. Sometimes it comes as a rude shock to learn that the sacrifice consists not in giving themselves up but in helping their children to give *them* up, this despite the ambivalence that many kids have about growing up.

3. Failing to Parent. Just because much of your child's adolescence has already been predetermined by her childhood doesn't mean that you can fold your tent and head happily into the sunset. Your teenager still requires a lot of parental support, guidance, *and* discipline. But it will be harder now, because your teenager will never admit that you're right and she's wrong, she will shrug off any attempts on your part to be affectionate with her, and she will act as if she's catatonic and can't hear a word you're saying. But letting go too soon can be just as devastating to your teenager as not letting go soon enough. And divorce has made this an even more critical issue than ever before, as we'll discuss in the next chapter.

4. Failing to Respect Your Teenager's Privacy. Snooping around your teenager's bedroom, "accidentally" eavesdropping on his phone conversations, and reading her secret diary are all common parental behaviors that are fraught with hazard. Yes, you want to know what is happening in their lives; and no, they won't always be willing to volunteer much information. Your teenager's desire for privacy may seem excessive or at times even prudish, but respecting this need demonstrates your respect for your teenager's having a life of his own.

5. Depriving Teenagers of the Easy Symbols of Their Adolescence. For reasons beyond my understanding, many parents believe that if their teenager goes to school in torn jeans, or with green spiked hair, it "reflects back on them." Stuff and nonsense! You can't afford to have an identity crisis at the same time as your teenager. Be assured that if your teenager chooses to look like a slob, it reflects back on no one other than her. Consequently, it's *her* problem, not yours.

6. *Succumbing to Peer Pressure Yourself.* Teenagers aren't the only ones subjected to peer pressure. Adults are notoriously susceptible to it. For example, does this sound familiar? "Hi, how are you? Welcome to the party. Can I get you a drink?" Or, in some social circles: "Honey, Brian's going to be sixteen, and he's such a good kid. Don't you think we should get him his own car? The Wilsons bought Doug a car when he turned sixteen." Don't *ever* let your kids talk you into or out of something simply because "everyone else is doing it." That is precisely the kind of peer pressure that they are susceptible to but to which you, as an adult, should be immune.

7. *Overestimating the Peer Group's Influence and Underestimating Your Own.* Particularly when things go wrong, it's easy to blame your teenager's peers. I've heard many statements from parents like "Oh, Barbara's basically a good kid, but she's gotten mixed up with a very tough crowd" and "It's those darn kids that Jake hangs around with—he'd never do something like this on his own." Very similar to a popular expression in our childhood: Flip Wilson's "The Devil made me do it." But the peer group is analogous to a hypnotist—it can't make your child do anything that's fundamentally against his will. If you've raised him properly up until age twelve, it's unlikely that the peer group will be able to overcome that influence, no matter how powerful it is. In addition, it's even more likely that your child will select a peer group that shares many of his own values in the first place.

Parents often mistakenly think that they have lost control of their child, simply because she is now a teenager. In trying to hold intelligent conversations with teenagers, parents are mistaking style for substance. Yes, your teenager *acts* as if he is not listening to a word you're saying. In that sense, teenagers *are* like catatonic schizophrenics, who, in their stupor, can be positioned this way or that way, without any apparent recognition or acknowledgment of you by them. But once they break out of their stupor, catatonic patients can repeat word for word what you told them two months ago. And teenagers can, too. Better yet, they often know what you are going to say, or think, in any given situation without your even being there. That's because you've trained them properly!

Believe it or not, your teenagers really do listen when you tell them something. They *have to*—you are their "superego." On the other hand, they do not always have to *acknowledge* to you that they have been listening, nor do they necessarily have to follow your instructions to the letter. However, if you make the mistake of thinking your kids aren't listening and consequently don't even make the effort to talk with them, you are depriving your teenagers of your help and guidance at a very crucial time. By discussing important topics, you are forcing your kids to at least incorporate your attitudes and beliefs into their own emerging set of standards. Even if they don't agree with you, they will have to wrestle with the differences between your system and theirs and somehow explain the discrepancy to themselves—but *only* if you discuss things with them. Otherwise, their internal theme song becomes Cole Porter's tune, "Anything Goes."

❑ ❑ ❑

Take a unique psychology, add a combination of unique growth and development, and top it off with a heavy dose of Western culture and you've got the fundamental reasons why teenagers can be difficult people to deal with or try to parent. Worse yet, they themselves are only vaguely aware of the idiosyncrasies of their thinking and behavior. But you, smart parent that you are, now have the upper hand. If you can't outsmart them, at least you can understand what they are going through and how they are thinking. And as they mature, most adolescents outgrow many of their idiosyncrasies, and they are capable of responding to at least some parental guidance. In a later chapter we will discuss what strategies you can use to help guide your teenagers through their adolescence with a minimum of trauma, to yourselves and them. But next, let's take a look at why both parents and teenagers are more stressed today than ever before, and what you can do about it.

Chapter 2

The Next Generation: New Stresses, New Strategies

❑

Although each generation tends to think of itself as unique and living in the most difficult of times (for example, Thomas Paine's "These are the times that try men's souls"), times *have* changed, and not necessarily for the better. For baby boomers, the threat to world peace was omnipresent. Now the threats are closer to home. No previous generation of teenagers had to confront anything even remotely like the Human Immunodeficiency Virus (HIV). No previous generation saw so many young people exposed to alcohol, cigarettes, pregnancy, sexually transmitted diseases, suicide, and violence. In medicine there is an ancient saying, "Desperate diseases require extreme remedies." The time has come for extreme remedies—new strategies to combat the new stresses that our teenagers must confront almost daily.

THE AT-RISK GENERATION

Consider the following information, from the 1989 National Adolescent Student Health Survey (NASHS), which surveyed more than eleven thousand eighth- and tenth-grade students in twenty states:

- Fifty-six percent of the students had not worn a seat belt that last time they rode in a car. Forty-four percent had ridden with a driver who had used alcohol or drugs before driving.
- Half of the boys and more than one-fourth of the girls had been involved in at least one physical fight in the previous year.
- Twenty-five percent of the girls reported that someone had tried to force them to have sexual relations during the past year.
- Twenty-three percent of the boys reported having carried a knife at least once in the past year, and 7 percent daily. Nearly two-thirds reported having used a gun, for any reason.
- Forty-two percent of the girls and 25 percent of the boys reported having seriously considered suicide at some time, and 18 percent of the girls and 11 percent of the boys had actually made suicide attempts.
- More than 60 percent of the girls had dieted during the past year. Sixteen percent had used diet pills, 12 percent had induced vomiting, and 8 percent had used laxatives.
- Nearly half of all the students surveyed thought that donating blood increased the likelihood of becoming infected with HIV, and more than half were unsure or believed that "washing after having sex" decreased the likelihood of infection.

Despite these noticeable threats to adolescent health, an average of only one-third to one-half of teenagers had received any instruction in school about these major health issues. The notable exception was for alcohol and drugs: Nearly 90 percent of students reported having been exposed to school programs. Clearly, the "just say no" mentality is alive and well in the United States; and, just as clearly, it will not protect teenagers against some of the most significant threats to their health and well-being.

Many adults don't like it when I say that our kids have it tougher today than we did when we were growing up. For some reason (human nature, probably), we like to think that we have suffered more than anyone else, and that our kids have it easy and are spoiled rotten. Materially, that may be true. Today's kids have an incredible amount of spending power, and they use it—to the tune of $70 billion a year (a figure not lost on Madison Avenue advertisers or MTV). But just as Madonna sings in "Material Girl," today's children and teenagers do not derive as much satisfaction from material objects as they do from the same "basics" that we wanted when we were growing up: love, security, respect, etc.

Making it even more difficult for parents and children to cope is the fact that the American family has changed. "Father knows best" is an anachronism: Father may not even be around, much less paying child support, and he and Mother may never have gotten married in the first place. More likely than not, Mother has a job and therefore has to rely on relatives or day care to help with the children. It seems ironic that despite the end of the cold war, the world is a more dangerous place for our children to grow up in, and our families provide less of a safe haven than ever before. Think about the fact that as many as one-third of all American children have experienced their parents' divorce, and as many as half will spend part of their childhood with only one parent. More than two and a half million children have lost at least one parent through death. Each year, nearly 18 percent of children move with their families to a new home. An estimated 1 to 2 percent of children suffer physical or sexual abuse during their childhood.

TEENAGE SUICIDE

In fact, we have a chillingly accurate barometer of teenage stress in the 1990s: the suicide rate. Since 1960 the teen suicide rate has increased 300 percent. To put this number in perspective, in the United States an average of thirteen teenagers kill themselves *every day*. And for every completed suicide, there are an estimated one to two hundred failed attempts. Just walk into any high school classroom and ask the kids, "How many of you know someone who has either attempted suicide or actually committed suicide?" and virtually every hand will be raised. The same may be true for parents: How many of you haven't heard about a teenager who has attempted or succeeded in committing suicide? For many parents, the thought of teen suicide is an intense fear, especially when the number of arguments they're having with their kids seems to be increasing, or their teenager seems unusually moody and preoccupied. Why are kids doing this, and what does it tell us about modern adolescents' behavior?

As a matter of fact, more adults than adolescents kill themselves. But, as with many things (drugs, crime, sex), teenagers seem to attract most of the negative publicity. Also, among adolescents suicide is the third leading cause of death (after accidents and homicides), and it is the second leading cause of death among those aged fifteen to twenty-four. Several surveys have found that 12 to 42 percent of teens have some form of suicidal thoughts at any time.

Adolescent suicide is not only a tragedy, it seems to anger many adults—even health professionals who work with children and adolescents. They want to know how teenagers can "throw away their lives when they have so much to live for." Again, the uniqueness of adolescent thinking plays a key role here: Teenagers frequently do not have an adult, mature concept of death. The concepts of the imaginary audience and the personal fable lead some teens to fantasize about how sorry everyone will be after they're gone (of course, they'll be floating over their funeral, watching, as one teenager told me when he tried to explain why he was thinking of jumping out of a third-story window at school after his girlfriend broke up with him). In one study of nearly six hundred thirteen- to sixteen-year-olds, researchers found that 20 percent thought that they would still be "alive" after death, 60 percent envisioned some sort of spiritual continuation, and only 20 percent viewed death as total cessation. In other words, many teenagers attempt suicide because they do not have a mature, realistic, adult view of life and death. Given their limited life experience, this should not surprise us.

How Adults Misunderstand Teen Suicide

There are many misconceptions about teen suicide. The most dangerous is that there is a difference between "gestures" and "attempts." The word "gesture" is somehow meant to trivialize the teenager's attempt: She swallowed only a handful of pills, so she "wasn't really trying" to kill herself. Wrong. The only reason she didn't kill herself was that she didn't have the lethal means available—a gun. *All suicide attempts are serious and are meant to be taken seriously.*

A second common misconception is that if you ask a teenager if he is thinking about committing suicide, somehow you'll put an idea into his head that wasn't there before. This is analogous to the "if you teach kids about sex, they'll go out and do it" school of thought—as if you're giving them an idea that they haven't already thought about for twenty-six hours a day (if they're young and male). But, as we've just seen, a sizable number of teenagers have thought about suicide at one time or another. Asking them about it may *prevent* a suicide, not cause one.

The final misconception that bears correcting is that one perpetrated by the National Rifle Association: "Guns don't kill people; people kill people." *Much of the increase in the teenage suicide rate can be blamed directly on the increased production, sale, and availability of handguns in the United States.* In one study, half of all male adolescents owned a gun. And, as hard to believe as this may seem, in another study one-fourth of attempters reported that their families continued to keep a firearm in the house even following their attempt!

Who Commits Suicide and Why?

Most teenagers who commit suicide can be identified ahead of time. About 50 percent have had a long history of school and behavioral problems, including fighting at school and with parents; about 20 to 25 percent are depressed; and 1 to 2 percent are psychotic. The ones who scare the hell out of every parent and pediatrician are the 20 to 25 percent who are "model teenagers," often with good grades, who have never been any trouble to their parents and frequently are admired as "ideal kids." However, beneath the surface these are often anxious, perfectionistic, rigid teenagers who are facing an acute and humiliating loss. It can be the breakup of a relationship, their parents' divorce, the loss of self-esteem after being ridiculed by friends, or it can be the loss of a good grade on a test, or the death of a close friend, a family member, or even a pet. Many teens commit suicide in the interval between this loss and the impending humiliation or disciplinary action, and that interval can be extremely brief. Alcohol and other drugs are a frequent accompaniment and may also be partially responsible for the increase in suicide rates in the past three decades. Finally, adolescents who have been sexually abused are at three times as great a risk of committing suicide, and gay teenagers may have an increased risk as well.

What is imperative to understand here is that teenagers who commit suicide often do it impulsively—because things seem irretrievably bleak—and because the means to kill themselves is at hand: a handgun. Take the gun out of the house and you've got a kid who takes a handful of aspirin and survives, rather than one with a bullet in his head who dies. These may be harsh words, but they are absolutely true. Handguns represent one of the biggest public health menaces to children and teenagers today—a far greater threat than measles or meningitis or cancer. And once a teenager makes a suicide attempt, he has a 1 to 9 percent chance of eventually succeeding in future attempts.

Attempters Versus Completers

What distinguishes the successful from the unsuccessful attempters? Teenagers who kill themselves often have a history of psychological disturbance and previous attempts, and they have a strong desire to die, as manifested by their timing the suicide to avoid discovery, their choice of a lethal method, and their proclaiming ahead of time their intent to die. Teens who make unsuccessful attempts may be experiencing *conflict* in their lives more than an acute loss. This can include conflict with a parent or friend, or physical or sexual abuse. When normal teen- agers are surveyed about what they find stressful in their lives, they report a surprising number of negative events (according to a study of 172 eleven- to nineteen-year-olds in Nashville, Tennessee, reported in *Pediatrics*, 75:19, 1985):

Failing grades on report card	34%
Increased arguments between parents	28%
Serious family illness	28%
Broke up boyfriend/girlfriend	24%
Death in family	22%
Problem with siblings	21%
Teacher problems	14%
Parents divorced	13%
Death of a close friend	11%

Again, because of the uniqueness of adolescents' think- ing, certain setbacks that adults would easily shrug off become life-threatening: receiving a B on an exam instead of an A, not making the cheerleading squad, etc. One of my favorite patients, whom I saw in counseling for several months, attempted suicide after having had an abortion— not because the abortion was upsetting her but because several of her friends had found out about it! An estimated two-thirds of teen suicide attempters *do not want to die*. Rather, they make very impulsive attempts, seeking to communicate their anger or frustration, or to escape what seems like an impossible situation. This may be where the concept of a "gesture," or "cry for help," comes from. Simply put, teenagers do not have the coping skills, the communication skills, or the long-range perspective on

life of most adults. If teenagers could verbalize their feelings—for example, "My parents are divorcing, and I feel
that it is my fault"—they would be adults, not teenagers.
Yet, in fact, many adults cannot express their true "gut"
feelings about what is happening to them either. Blaming
teenagers for their emotional immaturity and their inabil-
ity to communicate effectively is simply unfair and counterproductive.

Preventing Teen Suicide

In an attempt to prevent the well-publicized suicide "clus-
ters" among teenagers, educators have intensified their
school-based efforts. However, such efforts may vary
greatly in their quality and effectiveness. Suicide-preven-
tion programs in schools should teach all of the following
concepts:

- Suicide is a permanent solution to a temporary problem that can be improved.
- Death is permanent and final and does not allow the
teenager any satisfaction from whatever ensues afterward.
- Suicidal thoughts are common, but if they persist,
help should be sought.
- People who commit suicide are dysfunctional and,
sadly, lack the ability to find help for problems that
usually are solvable.

TEENAGERS AND MODERN STRESSES

Clearly, American teenagers are stressed, and they are
communicating their stress loudly, clearly, and dysfunc-
tionally. But attempting or committing suicide is not the
only way teenagers are telling us how much they are hurt-

ing. Steadily climbing rates of teenage sexual activity and drug use since the 1970s may represent a feedback phenomenon: While some teenagers use drugs or sex to relieve their tensions, many others see the allegedly high rates of sexual intercourse and drug use among their peers and feel that they are the "last American virgin" or the only kid in America who hasn't tried beer by age fifteen. All of the publicity surrounding teenagers' behavior—and sex, drugs, and rock 'n' roll always draw big headlines—may, *in itself*, be stressful to teenagers.

Imagine, if you will, that you are a carpenter. Virtually every week your local newspaper has an article on how many carpenters are having nervous breakdowns. Cover stories in *Time* and *Newsweek* discuss prominent carpenters who have gone berserk. *60 Minutes* does an exposé on the poor quality of mental health services for psychotic carpenters. At cocktail parties, people constantly stare at you or come up to you and ask, "How *are* you?" You get the idea.

DIVORCE: A MODERN REALITY

❑

ALISON: Alison B. is a very precocious thirteen-year-old whose mother phones to ask if they can both come to talk with me. Mrs. B. is worried that, although Alison has been in "gifted" classes for many years and is a straight-A student, her grades now are beginning to decline and she says she "doesn't care anymore." In addition, Mrs. B. discovered that a bottle of whiskey was missing from the liquor cabinet and found it, empty, in the back of Alison's closet. When she confronted Alison, the response was "I don't know how it got there . . . bottles don't have legs, do they?" Mrs. B. is also concerned that their relationship has deteriorated in the past year and that they argue all the time.

When they arrive, Alison is sullen and angry and speaks in monosyllables. Her mother is an attractive thirty-two-year-old, bright and college-educated, and very successful working as a realtor. Alison's father, a lawyer, lives a thousand miles away; her parents have been divorced for two years. She is an only child. She usually gets to spend either Christmas or spring vacation with him, and they talk on the phone about once a month. For the past six months Mrs. B. has been dating a man named Paul, who has recently begun spending the night. Alison and Paul "are like oil and water," according to her mother.

After talking to them together, I ask to speak with Alison alone. I tell her that I don't blame her for being angry with her mother for dragging her to see me—I'd feel the same way if her mother dragged me to see a stranger. She smiles slightly. I also tell her that she doesn't have to talk with me if she doesn't want to. She resists making eye contact but begins answering my questions with more than monosyllables. School is "boring." Her mother "cares about nothing except her work" and is "never around." She and her best friend got drunk one afternoon after school, and her mother didn't even suspect anything was wrong when she came home at 10 P.M. and Alison was asleep on top of her bed, with her clothes still on. Then, a week later, her mother searched her room without her permission, "a real Nazi move." She has never had sexual intercourse, although she has her eyes on "a guy who's a real hunk." She quickly looks at me to see my reaction. Occasionally she thinks about killing herself, although she doesn't really know how she'd do it and she hates the sight of blood, especially her own. She always used to think that she wanted to become a lawyer, but *now she's not so sure. She'd like to move to Florida to live with her father, but she's afraid that "he won't have time for me either." At this point her eyes fill with tears.*

❏

If growing up is more difficult today than ever before, so is parenting, and for many of the same reasons. Not only are the times different, and families different, but our responses to important subjects like sex and drugs also are different. When we were growing up, if we had ten good friends, maybe *one* would have been in Alison's situation. What has happened to the "traditional American family"? During the Eisenhower and Kennedy years (when you and I were kids), it seemed that no one was divorced. The concept of a stepparent was about as foreign as E.T. Now, with some families, you need a scorecard to keep track of who's who. The nuclear family is obviously deteriorating. (Perhaps it's called "nuclear" because it's beginning to look as if a nuclear bomb has been dropped on the average American family.)

According to a new study by Dennis Ahlburg and Carol De Vita at the Population Reference Bureau, one in three Americans is currently part of a stepfamily; and by the year 2000, *half* of all Americans will be part of a stepfamily (Richard Chin: "Stepfamilies May Be Half of United States by 2000," Knight-Ridder Newspapers, August 26, 1992).

Here's another, older teenager's account (published in *Parade* magazine, April 28, 1991). Stephanie, age nineteen, lives in Evansville, Indiana:

> "When I was 15, my parents separated, and it was devastating for me. It's been four years since then, and I still feel the same way I did the day I found out. I can remember the day I came home and found my mom lying there

on the couch, looking sick. When she told me, my heart just dropped. I was very close to my father, so I felt abandoned and alone. I thought, 'How could you leave me and Leigh?' (My younger sister was 8 then.)

"It's hard for me to forgive my father. He married a good friend of my mom's and moved in with her and her three children—twin boys my age and a son three years younger. I live on my own now, and they get a lot of things I don't get. It's real hard.

"We lived in a small town where everybody knew about everything, and that kinda made it hard too. We tried family therapy, but that didn't accomplish anything, so our feelings were never spoken about after that.

"I feel like a stranger in my father's home. Dad always says it's my home too, but I just don't feel right over there. I feel real left out. I know my father doesn't want me to feel that way, but I'm always thinking about what we used to do and what we don't do now. We always used to go on trips, and now my dad never takes my sister and me. He would, but he's always wanting to go with everybody, and I say, 'Why can't you just go with me and Leigh a couple of times?' But he doesn't want to do that. I don't want to go if it's going to be all of us, because then he won't talk to Leigh and me. Well, he'll talk to us, but not the way we used to talk. It's not the way it used to be."

Certainly, there are situations where divorce is either inevitable (the shotgun wedding resulting from teenage pregnancy) or even desirable (the abusive spouse). But I wonder if the current crisis in marriage isn't either because our own parents failed to parent us successfully (and stayed together "for the kids' sake") or—just the opposite —because they parented us too well, creating a model that none of us could hope to emulate.

Or is it because we really *are* a "me first" generation? We seem to be the first generation of adults that has a real sense of entitlement—"You only go around once in life, so grab for all you can," according to one well-known beer commercial. And that seems to be precisely what many of us are trying to do. As we'll see in a later chapter, the media may be affecting our expectations of each other and our sense of what our lives should be like. In other words, slowly and subtly, we've been conditioned by TV shows like *Cosby* and movies like *Pretty Woman* to expect that our spouse will always be our best friend and "be there for us," and that we'll all live happily ever after, without too many problems that can't be easily solved, especially if we throw enough money at them. So when real life intervenes with mortgages and car payments and arguments over who's going to wash the dishes or change the baby's diaper, we have a very hard time handling it—and each other.

Another possible reason for the high divorce rate could be that we have lost our sense of permanence in the world. Ours is the first generation of kids who grew up periodically tucking our heads between our legs in nuclear war drills. While other generations have certainly had to face the specter of war, none has had to cope with the threat of nuclear war. And studies show that we thought about it and worried about it quite a lot.

Despite the perceived trauma of divorce, many kids seem to cruise right through their parents' divorce. Such children and teenagers may be extremely adaptable, or their parents may be extremely sensitive to their children's needs as well as their own, or the kids may recognize that both parents are more pleasant to be with now that they are separated. However, the last situation represents an area of great controversy. Some experts estimate that divorce is a "positive experience" for only 10 percent of kids exposed to it, even when their parents had been physically abusive to each other. On the other hand, a study published in *Science* in 1991 examined more than twenty thousand children and found that many problems arise during the period before the divorce actually occurs, when the family is dysfunctional because of parental conflict. In one excellent study of normal children and adolescents, 37 percent still showed signs of moderate to severe depression five years after their parents' breakup.* School problems, peer problems, sexual acting out, preoccupation with divorce—the manifestations can range from subtle to obvious.

Remember the giant redwood forest? Imagine that it is being totally obliterated right in front of your eyes, and you are only five years old. Children of divorcing parents often experience a variety of emotions, ranging from anxiety and sorrow to anger and guilt. In particular, they may feel suddenly "exposed" and extremely vulnerable. Children frequently blame themselves for a parent's departure. However, they certainly do not necessarily wear such emotions on their sleeve. Parents divorcing is probably the single greatest stress that most children ever face.

Minimizing the Effects of Divorce

How to lessen the impact of divorce is a complex subject that is probably beyond the scope of this book, but I should at least mention a few basic principles:

- Telling children about an impending divorce is not the sort of news accomplished in a single, grand announcement. Rather, it should be the beginning of a supportive process of helping the child understand

* This study and much of the ensuing discussion is derived from the work of Dr. Judith Wallerstein. (See appendix I.)

the rationale for the divorce and how her life will continue to proceed in a different but orderly fashion.

- Children need to know what divorce means, and what changes they can expect in their everyday lives.
- Most importantly, children need to know that they are not being abandoned, that both parents still love them and will take care of them, and that the parent-child relationships will proceed as normally as before.
- Children need to be reassured that they are *not* the cause of their parents' divorce, that what their parents are doing has been considered carefully, and that attempts to remain together have failed. Similarly, children need to understand that, just as they did not cause the divorce, neither can they mend the marriage sometime in the future.
- Children should be given permission to experience whatever they are feeling about the divorce.
- The golden rule of divorce: *At no time should a child be caught in the cross fire between parents.*

Divorce and Child Rearing

As we'll discuss later, the single most stress-producing problem for newly divorced parents is discipline. At precisely the time when consistency in discipline is most crucial, parents are prone to be most lax, because they themselves feel vulnerable and out-of-control. This compromises their ability to parent and makes them more susceptible to their kids' criticism or reproaches. Single mothers in particular have problems in their new role of full-time disciplinarian. Kids, on the other hand, are quick to detect their parents' weaknesses. After all, if you had two bosses and desperately wanted a pay raise, wouldn't you try both bosses before settling for nothing? Most children are supreme opportunists and do this sort of thing all the time, even when their parents aren't divorced. As in all other parenting situations, firmness and consistency are the two paramount virtues.

With divorce and with many other common but taxing parenting situations, parents need to realize that they have a strong ally: their pediatrician. Increasingly young pediatricians are being trained to deal not only with strep throat and diaper rash but with psychosocial issues as well. Yet most parents don't seem to know that they can rely on their pediatrician to help assess these sorts of complex problems and either counsel children themselves or know where to refer them. (More about this later.)

THE CHANGING INTACT AMERICAN FAMILY

Divorce isn't the only culprit. The feminist movement has helped to change the American family as well—in ways that are both good and not so good. Women are no longer the "happy homemakers" they once were. They have nearly as much of a chance at having a career as men do. But the down side is that they are no longer so available for child-rearing duty.

When we adopted our son, I stayed at home with him for a month. If I had had more paternity leave than that, I would have needed a lobotomy. As a pediatrician, I have a tremendous amount of admiration and respect for women who stay home to raise their children. But as someone who likes to think of himself as an intelligent human being, I can say only that such behavior is beyond both my capacity and my abilities. For women, the decision to stay home with the kids or arrange for day care is extraordinarily difficult, and I don't have any easy advice on the subject. Staying home with your kids is obviously a great idea from *their* point of view. But, at the same time, it does increase the risk that they will grow up with a Ptolemaic view of the world. Also, if your mental health is going to be jeopardized because you're not in your office five days a week, furthering your career, or if you're like me and don't have the temperament to be a full-time baby sitter, then by all means don't do it! I'd much prefer a happy, well-adjusted mother spending evenings and weekends with her kids than a neurotic and angry mother being home all day every day.

Unfortunately, according to popular psychologist John Rosemond and others, we still live in a "single-parent culture." This applies even if you are happily married. What does he mean by this?* For some reason, feminism has not liberated women from the notion that their children's fate determines their own. Women continue to define themselves in terms of their children: how well their kids are doing in school, what clothes they wear, their after-school activities. A mother's self-image seems much more intricately linked with whether her child is doing well than is the father's. Modern women are still led to believe that their primary responsibility, even if they work full time, is to see that their children's needs are always fulfilled. Not only is this dangerous—since children inevitably must learn about unhappiness and frustration, and preferably early in their young lives—it is unfair to women in general. Consider this example from John Rosemond's syndicated column:

---

* For more about this line of reasoning, see Dr. John Rosemond's book, listed in appendix I. (John Rosemond, a psychologist in private practice in Gastonia, NC, is a syndicated weekly newspaper columnist and featured Parent Columnist for *Better Homes and Gardens* magazine. He is the author of *Parent Power!*, *John Rosemond's Six-Point Plan for Raising Happy, Healthy Children*, and *Ending the Homework Hassle*, Andrews & McMeel, $8.95).

A mother recently told me she absolutely hated the "scene" at after-school sports events, but her 10-year-old wanted to play soccer. I suggested she could make him responsible for that decision by taking him to the games and dropping him off with a wish that he have fun.

"But that would hurt his feelings," she said.

"Meaning?" I asked.

"I mean he'd be disappointed if I wasn't there to watch him play."

"But you told me you don't want to be part of what's going on in the stands," I reminded. "Believe me, he can survive his mother not doing something he wants her to do."

Her gaze misted over and became distant. Finally, in the softest of voices, she said, "But I just can't bring myself to do something that would make him upset."

All of this would be academic if we had the kind of government and society that really recognized the importance of early child-rearing. I am not trying to be political here, but governmental policies affect the way we raise our kids. Nearly every Western nation allows one parent, if not both, six months to two years' leave for child rearing. In most cases this is *paid* leave. Contrast this with the fact that in 1990 President Bush vetoed a parental leave bill passed by Congress that would simply have guaranteed that a person's job would not be lost if she took six weeks of unpaid leave! I am not speaking here as either a Democrat or a Republican but as an advocate for children and teenagers and their parents. One noted American pediatrician has wondered out loud if there isn't an actual conspiracy against children in our country. On an individual and family level, we seem to treasure our children (perhaps even too much); but on a societal level, we do as little as we possibly can. Children inevitably lose out to defense spending, Social Security, and financing the national debt. Perhaps if our government did more for children—such as Head Start, day care, parental leave, financial support for schools—we parents wouldn't have to worry about our children so much.

With 60 percent of the nation's women now gainfully employed, who *is* minding the children? You might think —and rightfully so—that it is the *father's* responsibility as well as the mother's to raise their kids and therefore we should begin to see a large increase in househusbands. Not on this planet, dude. The male's role in society as hunter and provider has been established through thousands of years, and it's not about to change in a few brief generations. High-quality day care is essential, but in the U.S. Government's list of priorities it seems to rank just below refurbishing Lawrence Welk's boyhood home and about twenty places below continuing to fund the Strategic Defense Initiative ("Star Wars").

The Myth of "Quality Time"

One of the most pervasive myths of our society is the notion of "quality time." Parents used to spend a lot of time with their kids. They enjoyed it, mostly. But then things changed. Some parents found that they needed more and more-expensive material things to keep themselves happy. Others found that they just couldn't keep up even their ordinary standard of living on one salary. So they decided to work even harder, and in some families both parents decided that they needed to work outside the home. Experts in child care objected, but they didn't want to make parents feel *too* guilty, so the concept of "quality time" evolved—if you can't spend enough time with your kids, you can at least rationalize it by saying that the time you do spend is extra special and therefore should count double. Talk about "spin control"! This sounds like something that only Lee Atwater or Madison Avenue could dream up. The only trouble is, it's total nonsense. Worse than that, it's potentially counterproductive to good relations with your kids.

Why? First of all, important things happen with kids at random or odd moments, not in glorious epiphanies (the way it happens on TV or in the movies). Think of it in terms of probability theory: If you want to see your one-year-old take his first steps, you can't schedule yourself an afternoon off from work and let him know that it's time for the big event. It's simply a matter of the more time that you're at home, the greater the likelihood that you'll see it happen. My father used to wait for moments when we were alone together—his idea of "quality time"—to start his "Son, are there any questions you have about sex?" lecture. Consequently, I used to try to avoid being alone with him. He would have been far more successful if he had seized a moment that was more appropriate— an off-color joke that someone else had told, a particularly sexy billboard ad, anything.

Second, parents who subscribe to the "quality time" myth tend either to spoil or to overwhelm their children. As one expert, Dr. George Comerci, observes (in *Adolescent Medicine: State of the Art Reviews*, June 1991):

> Children should be made to feel wanted, loved, and valued but not possessed, overprized, or indulged. They should be expected to perform well, not for their parents' fulfillment and satisfaction and that of others, but rather for their own gratification, inner satisfaction, pride, and sense of accomplishment. Parents must be there, accessible, accepting, and available (the three "A"s of good parenting . . .) but cannot become subservient to or totally

enmeshed in the lives of their children. That winding and difficult path between overinvolvement on one side and apathy or [uninterest] on the other is a difficult one for parents to follow.

Teenagers, of course, are especially unlikely either to appreciate such tactics or to be vulnerable to them. The less time spent with you the better, so far as they are concerned.

But there is simply no substitute for time spent with your kids, particularly in their early childhood and pre-teen years. Granted, some parents have no choice, and others have excellent day-care arrangements (such as Grandma). But the idea that "quality" can make up for "quantity" is a very sad delusion in our society. Besides, all "quantity" time *should* be "quality time" anyway. Yet in one study American fathers were found to spend an average of two minutes a day in actual one-to-one conversation with any of their children! Meanwhile, American children spend four to five hours a day camped in front of the television set.

Clearly, the American family is changing in a number of profound and potentially unhealthy ways. One of my favorite *New Yorker* cartoons shows a mother and father walking down the street with their brood of children. Half the children are wearing T-shirts that say "His," the other half T-shirts that say "Hers." Another favorite cartoon shows a child parked in front of the TV set with a beer in hand. The mother looks at the father and says, "No, I thought he was *yours*." It is hard enough being a parent—being a stepparent only complicates the process. And human nature tells us that older children and teenagers will always try to get the best deal they can, from whichever parent is willing to give in to them.

❑

CAROL: Carol D. is a sixteen-year-old whose mother brings her to see me because she suspects that Carol is having sex with her boyfriend and is using drugs. Mrs. D. is in her early forties and works as a paralegal at a large downtown firm. She carries herself with an air of authority and competence. She has been divorced for five years and has a younger son, Jimmy, age eleven. A week ago Carol was given permission to sleep over at her girlfriend's house. When Mrs. D. called there, Carol was not around or expected. When confronted by her mother, Carol refused to say where she had been. In addition, Carol's grades have fallen from A's and B's to C's and D's.

Alone, Carol is a strong-willed and somewhat hostile young woman who readily admits to sleeping with her boyfriend and to using a variety of drugs, including alcohol, marijuana and cocaine. She is not using any contraception but would be interested in birth control pills, so long as her mother doesn't find out. When asked about sex, she says that her mother sleeps with a variety of men, so why shouldn't she? She sees nothing wrong with using drugs and plans to continue. They make her "feel good" and "help me forget." Besides, she angrily points out, her mother smokes two packs of cigarettes a day and frequently comes home looking hungover the morning after a date. Carol's best friend, Jacki, is her source of drugs: Jacki steals some marijuana or cocaine from her mother's supply, kept in a bedroom closet. Jacki and Carol also like to watch the "dirty movies" that Jacki's parents have collected. Some of the films include homemade footage of her parents snorting cocaine and then making love.

❑

Parents Growing Up

There is a cynical joke among many parents of teenagers that perhaps a contraceptive agent should be added to the drinking water. Married adults would then have to apply to a screening agency for the antidote before they could become parents. You'd be surprised at how much support you could get for this sort of idea! To paraphrase one of Shakespeare's famous passages from *Twelfth Night*: Parenthood is something that some are born to, some grow into, and some have thrust upon them. Unfortunately, the latter two groups may not be serving as very appropriate role models for their children, and role modeling is a crucial process in parenting. As James Baldwin wrote, "Children have never been very good at listening to elders, but they have never failed to imitate them."

One of the things that is new and different about parenting in the 1990s is that one or both parents may be experiencing their own delayed adolescence. Study after study documents that if parents use drugs, their children will likely use drugs—again, the crucial influence of role modeling. And there is no more important role in the world than that of parent. But, like Carol's mother and Jacki's parents, some people don't take that role very seriously. Or, worse yet, they want their kids to "do as I say, not as I do." Your children are far too perceptive to fall for an approach like that.

Kids like Carol and Jacki are being forced to grow up too fast. Some may be forced into an actual reversal of roles, so that the teenager has to parent the mother or father who is experiencing adolescent-type romances. Often such parents need their teenager to be a friend to them, which represents a major breach of contract. In his book *The Hurried Child* Elkind describes the three-part contractual process between parent and child: (1) freedom granted by parents, in return for responsibility demonstrated by the child or adolescent, (2) commitment by the parents, in return for loyalty, and (3) parental support, both emotional and economic, as an acknowledgment of achievement. He describes a breach of contract as one of the prime sources of alienation among youth:

> Given a society that puts emphasis on early achievement, when parents do not couple demands for that [early] achievement with a comparable level of support, there is disequilibrium in a parent-child contract. . . . As adolescents, these children pay their parents back for what they experienced as childhood inequities. Some young people direct their anger outward and engage in activities that hurt them and that are designed to hurt the parents as well. They may begin to do poorly in school, and may drop out entirely.

Radical Parents

With some parents, however, things are not as black-and-white: They *do* function as appropriate role models, but they also remember their heyday, back in the sixties, when they were campus radicals. And so they give their kids mixed messages about important things like sex and drugs. As we'll see in the next few chapters, if you don't want your kids to have sex until they're thirty, you must *say so*. It doesn't mean that that's what they'll decide to do, but at least they will have to wrestle with your values and advice. If you don't want your kids to use drugs, you will have to be very clear on the subject and spell out what the repercussions would be if they ever did. I can't tell you how many well-meaning parents I have seen over the past twelve years who tell their kids to "just say no" to drugs and then acquiesce in buying a keg of beer for a sixteenth-birthday party, or smile at their son when he comes home drunk for the first time.

The mixed message doesn't necessarily have to be about sex and drugs, either. It can involve respect for authority. A teenager gets her first speeding ticket, or is caught shoplifting, or tells a teacher to go to hell; if a parent, upon hearing about the episode, smiles and fondly remembers his own adolescence, all is lost. There is a crucial difference between tolerating (or expecting) certain behavior and *sanctioning* it. And so, at times, some of your thoughts and reminiscences may have to be kept to yourself, for the good of your children.

I think we all suffer from our own mixed messages as well. Many of us waited until we were in our thirties or forties to have children, and we think of them as being very precious. But at the same time we think of our own lives and our own psychological development as being very precious too. Conflicts are inevitable. And, unfortunately, the unwritten parental contract states that adult personal development may have to be sacrificed—or, at the very least, put on hold—in the interests of child development. Of course, if you take this statement to its logical conclusion, we'd have both parents staying home with their children for the first five years of their lives.

The Myth of the "Democratic Family"

Now let's tackle another traditional parenting myth—the "democratic family"—and see how it can be uniquely stressful. During the sixties and seventies child-care experts touted the need for parents to listen to their children, to help them participate in the parenting process, and sometimes even to be good friends with their children. Nothing could be further from the truth. Perhaps that explains why some of us grew up to be lacking as parents. Kids need parents to be parents, not friends. Friends are considerably easier to find then parents. This means clear and concise messages that say "I am in charge here, not you. I will take care of your everyday needs and try to see that you are reasonably happy. And I'd like you to feel comfortable coming to me with whatever problems you may have. However, I will not always agree with everything you think or do what you want me to do. And I will always have the final say in decisions concerning you as long as you live in this household, although I will be happy to listen to your thoughts and ideas." The *Cosby* show has done some very nice variations on this theme. When the Huxtable children keep asking for more and more privileges, Cliff finally becomes exasperated with their refusal to take no for an answer. Finally he says, "Why? Because *I'm the dad*, that's why."

Likewise, in a married couple's life the *family unit*, not "the kids," needs to take precedence over all else. If the family revolves around the kids, then the kids will quickly learn that they are (and should always be) the center of attention. It's Copernicus versus Galileo all over again, and we already know how that one turned out. Inevitably, such kids will suffer from an exaggerated sense of self-importance. And, just as inevitably, they soon will become very difficult to discipline. This is not to say that you should ignore your kids or be indifferent to them. Rather, this is a plea to keep things in perspective. When the family unit comes first, the children actually feel *more* secure and loved, because the family unit is cherished above all else.

Now let's take a closer look at the Big Three stresses for both parents and teenagers—sex, drugs, and rock 'n' roll —and try to find out who is doing what and why, and then begin to discuss how we as parents might be able to help protect our children from these threats, some of which, in this era of AIDS, have become literally life-threatening.

Chapter 3

Everything You've Always Wanted to Know About Teen Sex But Were Afraid to Ask

❏

So far as most parents are concerned, sex is the worst part of adolescence.

❏

MARTI: Marti D. is thirteen years old and lives in the inner city. Her mother brings her to see me so I can "put her on the pill." Mrs. D. is twenty-nine years old and a single mother. She doesn't want "the same thing happening to Marti" that happened to her. Mrs. D. eventually completed high school through a GED program and works as a secretary in the hospital. She had planned to go to college.

When seen alone, Marti is a nervous, slightly immature young girl who only recently began menstruating. She is not sexually active, is not even dating, and says she is not interested in having sex until after she's married.

BENNETT: *Bennett R. is a sixteen-year-old who comes to see me because of recurring chest pains. They have been occurring almost daily for the past two months. He is worried that he is having a heart attack. On further questioning, Bennett reluctantly divulges that he is gay. He has been having a sexual relationship with a twenty-year-old man for the past two months, and is worried that his parents will kick him out of the house if they learn about it.*

DANA: *Dana K. is a fifteen-year-old girl whose family is in an acute crisis after her mother "accidentally" discovered her birth control pills under a pile of sweaters in her bedroom bureau drawer. She has been having intercourse with her boyfriend for the past six months and went to Planned Parenthood to obtain the pill before beginning sex. She feels that her mother has violated her privacy and can't be trusted. Her father refuses to allow her boyfriend (who is eighteen) in the house, or even talk to him. Her mother is more disappointed than angry, feels that she and Dana could "always talk about everything," and had hoped that Dana would wait at least until college, or afterward, before beginning to have sexual relations.*

❑

Face it, sex is far more complicated now than it was during the sixties: More teenagers are "doing it," the risks have increased dramatically, and the media are saturated with suggestiveness and innuendo. In the sixties sex was easier. It was forbidden, clandestine, and fun. Now it's out in the open and much more of a problem for everyone. AIDS and other STDs (sexually transmitted diseases), teenage pregnancy, and homosexuality were not publicly debated when we were growing up. Gonorrhea and syphilis were something you snickered about, diseases that the army made riotously funny training films about. Birth control pills had barely been developed. The sexiest things in the media were the lingerie ads. On television, Laura Petrie on *The Dick Van Dyke Show* was everyone's idea of a beautiful woman. Rock music lyrics were sometimes suggestive but not outrageously so, and four-letter words were *verboten* on TV, in the movies, or on the radio.

In the sixties our parents never talked to us about sex, and I think that much of our problem today stems from that fact. Since we learn most of how to parent from how our own parents raised us, in this particular instance, I am sorry to say, our own parents didn't do a very good job. So we took it upon ourselves to learn on our own. If you were male, the double standard made things easy: You were welcome to do anything and everything you could get away with, and there were no bad repercussions. If you were female, and you were unfortunate enough to wind up "in the family way," most likely you were shipped off to some faraway relative, had your baby, gave it up for adoption, and then got on with your life.

Marti, Bennett, and Dana are all typical teenagers from my practice. Believe it or not, there are still many teenagers even today who are not engaging in sexual intercourse. Others are, and with disastrous consequences, such as pregnancy, pelvic inflammatory disease, and AIDS. Still others are grappling with their sexual identities and are confused about whether they are gay, bi, or straight. Perhaps you can identify with these teenagers' parents, or maybe the idea of your fifteen-year-old's having sex doesn't bother you. If this is the case, then you're not like most parents of teenagers I know. Why? In our old age, are we becoming as prudish as our parents were? I don't think so. I think it's precisely because many of us experimented with sex at an early age that we know how problematic it can be. Our parents told us to wait until we were forty-two and married to start having sex, and, of course, we didn't believe them. So we had sex at fifteen or seventeen or twenty (or we waited, but we certainly had lots of friends who indulged)—and lo and behold, our parents were essentially right (even if it was for the wrong reasons—because they were so uptight about the subject that they couldn't even discuss it with us). Most of us *couldn't* handle sex at such a young age. It's only now, when we are parents ourselves, that we are willing to acknowledge that perhaps we might have made a mistake in beginning to have sexual intercourse at too young an age.

But apparently now it's too late. Millions of teenagers have followed our lead and begun having intercourse in their teens. How do we reverse the trend?

SEX EDUCATION AT HOME

How to Begin

Let's start with the million-dollar question: What do you do when your precocious eleven-year-old daughter sidles up to you and innocently asks, "Mom, did you and Dad have sex before you were married?" Possible responses to this question include:

"No, honey. We waited until we were married, just as we hope you will wait."

"It's none of your goddamn business, dear."

"Yes, we did. But it wasn't very much fun. We should have waited."

"Why do you ask?"

"Go ask you father. I'm busy."

This is a real poser. Ours is the first generation of parents whose truthful answer to the above question is more likely to be yes than no. On the other hand, it's real tough to preach no premarital sex to your kids when you indulged in it yourself. If you and your husband waited until you were married to begin having sex, and you never had sex with anyone else before then, you can answer the above question with a clear conscience.

For the other 99.9 percent of you out there, let's look at your options: lie, evade, or tell the truth. Children are unbelievably astute in detecting lies and evasion, so I would not recommend either. But telling the truth doesn't mean telling "the whole truth and nothing but the truth." Even if you had twenty lovers and your husband had forty-two and you both used to hang out at Plato's Retreat every weekend, your kids don't need (and certainly don't want and are not entitled to) all the gory details. A lot depends on what sort of standards you would like to see your children adopt. So, for instance, if you believe that premarital sex is okay in the context of a mature, committed relationship, you might say, "Yes, we did begin having sex. But we had dated for two years and were already making plans to get married. We were both twenty at the time." That sort of response would also work even if you believe that premarital sex is wrong, but in that case you could add, "We were probably foolish not to have waited." I can't tell you exactly what to say, because I don't know how *you* feel about sex. But I can tell you that, like Holden Caulfield in *The Catcher in the Rye*, most kids can spot a phony a mile away, so trying to cover up just won't work.

I can also tell you what I tell your kids as their physician: "Sex is a wonderful thing, but it carries with it certain risks. Sex can be a difficult thing to handle emotionally. It can complicate relationships. It can also expose you to a lot of diseases and to pregnancy. If you were to ask me, as your doctor, when you should begin having sex, I couldn't give you an exact answer. That's really something you need to discuss with your parents. Each person is different, and each person has to decide for himself or herself. I can tell you that, contrary to what you probably think, every one of your friends is *not* out there having sex all the time. And, purely from a medical point of view, I want you to know that having sex, as enjoyable as it is, carries risks. And those risks increase with each new partner you have sex with, and they certainly increase if you don't use birth control.''

So if your kids start asking you embarrassing questions, try using the situation as a starting point for discussing the entire subject of sex and when you think people are mature enough to engage in it. What you say is not nearly as important as the fact that you are willing to discuss the subject in the first place. That already puts you way ahead of your parents and makes it far more likely that your child will come to you with questions in the future.

Sex is a difficult topic to write about adequately because all of you are at different levels of understanding and acceptance. It would be like asking a grade-school teacher to try to teach a combined class of first- through twelfth-graders. But we children of the fifties and sixties probably do share a few common features: Our parents didn't talk to us about sex, our own sexual activity began in an era of repression and secrecy about sex (isn't it amazing to realize that *Playboy* magazine began publishing when we were kids?), we tend to be much more liberal about sex than our parents were, we know much more about contraception, and we're scared as hell about teenage pregnancy and AIDS.

Contraception: Eight Important Myths

For the sake of discussion, let's start with the "C" word, contraception. Here is the gist of a recent essay by Joan Beck, a syndicated columnist for the *Chicago Tribune*. The headline reads, "Handing Out Condoms in High School Encourages Teen Sex":

> . . . How can parents try to teach young teenagers moral values and counsel them against premature sexual activity for which they are probably not psychologically ready and which may have consequences for which they are unprepared? By giving out condoms—and at least tacit permission to be sexually active—the schools also will be making it harder than ever for girls to say no. . . .

It seems ironic that while parents accuse teenagers of being ignorant about sex (and to a great extent they are), they continue—like Joan Beck—to subscribe to several time-worn myths themselves:

1. *Making birth control readily available makes teenagers more likely to have sex.* Wrong. Making birth control readily available makes teenagers less likely to have babies! It's really that simple. As we will see, the decision about when to begin having sexual intercourse is a complex one for teenagers, but it certainly does *not* involve whether birth control is readily at hand. How do we know this? Because the great majority of teenagers do not use birth control at their first sexual encounter; in fact, it usually takes six to twelve months before they even begin to think about coming to see a physician for contraceptive services. To repeat, *the availability of birth control does not make teenagers sexually active at any earlier age, or more sex-*

ually promiscuous once they begin having sex. Parents and health professionals frequently think that there are three choices when a teenage girl begins having sex: She can become pregnant, she can use birth control, or she can stop. In fact, the last choice is not actually on the menu. For parents, the real dilemma is whether to allow their daughters access to birth control or to become grandparents. And I have yet to meet a parent who willingly chose the latter option over the former.

2. *Providing contraception for teenagers has done nothing to decrease the teenage pregnancy rate.* Incorrect. Estimates are that about half a million *additional* teenage pregnancies have been avoided by teenagers using a medically appropriate form of birth control.

3. *Birth control pills are dangerous.* Wrong. In fact, birth control pills are safest to use during the teen years. It's women in their thirties and forties who smoke who are most likely to have medical complications from taking the pill. In the entire world's medical literature, there is only *one* reported death of a teenager from taking birth control pills—and that was in 1968, involving a pill that was probably twice as potent as today's pills. By contrast, the risk of dying from pregnancy and childbirth is ten to twenty-five times as great as any risk posed by the pill. To put the entire issue into perspective, I tell my teenage patients that they have as much of a chance of dying from taking the pill as they do of having a Boeing 747 jet crash through the ceiling and land on their heads.

4. *Birth control pills cause cancer.* This is a serious distortion of medical knowledge. The pill may contribute, in some small way, to cervical cancer, but we now know that human papilloma virus (the virus found in venereal warts) plays a far more important role.

The exact relationship between the pill and breast cancer remains controversial—some studies show an association, others don't. But, in fact, the pill prevents two major forms of cancer in women: ovarian and uterine. And since ovarian cancer is a major killer, this is not just an academic consideration. So, overall, the pill probably *prevents* more cancer than it causes, if any.

5. *Parents should be notified if their teenagers seek contraceptive services.* This was one of Ronald Reagan's old notions—the so-called squeal rule—which would have mandated that family planning clinics "squeal" on their adolescent patients. Of course, Reagan's poor relationships with his own children are well known—and that is precisely the point. Teenagers from families in which communication about sexuality is poor are precisely those most likely to become sexually active at a young age. They are the ones who need confidential services the most. In addition, there is a genuine public health issue here: If you squeal on teenagers, they will never seek medical services. Then the teenage pregnancy rate would really skyrocket. (Every state in the union recognizes this fact, because there are laws which allow teenagers to get confidential health treatment for a suspected STD. Obviously, if your child had a serious STD, you'd probably want to know about it. But the overriding concern here is for the health of teenagers and their contacts—the public health—not your "rights" as a parent.)

6. *Teenagers don't need easy access to birth control: The fear of pregnancy or AIDS will stop kids from having sex.* As most adults realize, the urge to have sex can be powerful. And, as we've already seen, teenagers fear nothing: They think that they are invulnerable, that

"it can't happen to me." A survey from Johns Hopkins Medical School found that more than half of all teenage girls who were not using contraception believed that they would not or could not become pregnant. As a result, we have one million teenage pregnancies a year and teenagers are at the highest risk of any age group for acquiring an STD. The only thing that happens when you make birth control difficult for teenagers to obtain is that they become mothers and fathers, and you become grandmothers and grandfathers. Have a cigar.

7. *Teaching kids about sex, particularly in school sex ed programs, makes them* more *likely to begin having sex at a young age.* Wrong, wrong, *wrong!* This is the worst myth of all. How can we be so naïve? Does teaching kids about civics make them more likely to become state senators? Does teaching them about geography make them more likely to drop out of school to join an expedition to Antarctica? This myth is contrary to all of the basic principles of education in this country. Teaching kids about *anything* makes them understand it better and become more knowledgeable about it. Period. Besides, as we'll discuss further on, the quality of sex education in American schools is deplorable.

8. *Sex education programs make kids* less *likely to begin having sex at a young age.* Sadly, this is a myth as well. Sex education in school is not the panacea that everyone once hoped it would be. Partly this is because of the poor quality of most programs. But mostly it is because most sex ed programs are the "quick fix" type, lasting only a few hours during one semester, whereas parents, peers, and the media have a far more longstanding and powerful impact on kids' decisions about sex.

The Basics of Sex Education at Home

One of the qualities that baby boomers may share with their parents is that they too are afraid to talk about sex with their kids. Study after study has shown that American parents do not like to talk with their children or teenagers about sex. Because of this, American television has become the leading sex educator of children and adolescents today. And television is not teaching your kids the sorts of things that you want them to be learning: responsibility, abstinence, the difference between love and lust, the need to use effective birth control once they do begin having intercourse.

Only an estimated 25 percent of mothers talk to their daughters about sex, and that discussion rarely includes birth control. What role fathers play in any of this is a mystery, as is the nature of young males' sex education. If sex education does occur at home, the usual extent of it is that the eight-year-old child gets a little chat about "the basic plumbing." But your kids need more than that, and they need it from you, first and foremost. Although I am a firm believer in sex education in school, I am also convinced that it also should be taking place at home *first*. But too many of us subscribe wholeheartedly to myth number 7: Talking to kids about sex "gives them ideas." Do you really believe that they don't think about it before you bring up the subject? Wishful thinking. Teenagers are *always* thinking about or worrying about sex. Just as asking a depressed teenager if he has thought about suicide is not going to put an idea into his head that he hasn't already had, talking about sex is not going to make him any more likely at age thirteen to hop into bed with anyone he is attracted to.

Contrary to Ronald Reagan's theories of child rearing, many studies have documented that in families in which mothers feel that they can discuss sexual matters with their teenage daughters, the girls are less likely to begin having sex at a young age. Moreover, if the mother can discuss birth control as well, her daughter is more likely to contracept if she does begin having sex. This is a very important principle. It is perfectly possible to say the following to your teenage son or daughter: "Look, sex is a beautiful thing. But I think you should be finished with college [married/in a long-term, committed relationship/ over twenty-one—choose one or more] before beginning to have sex with anyone. However, I recognize that you are your own person and that either you may not agree with my advice or you may decide not to follow it. Therefore, I have to tell you that if you do start having sex, you had better use birth control each and every time."

This is not a double or mixed message. Quite the contrary—it is very clear: "Don't have sex when you're young, but if you do, use birth control." And it's a message that could literally save your child's life. I urge you to think about using it with your children and teenagers.

I can understand parents being nervous about giving their kids the wrong idea about sex. *Your* parents didn't do a very good job, and that makes it far more difficult on you. But somewhere along the line we've got to break the generational circle of noncommunication about this subject. Why? For one thing, it may be protective. For another, teenagers today are still incredibly ignorant about sexual matters. As Elizabeth Roberts, the author of "Teens, Sexuality, and Sex: Our Mixed Messages" (*Television and Children*, 1983), sadly notes:

I've often wondered what it would be like if we taught young people swimming the same way we teach sexuality. If we told them that swimming was an important adult activity, one they will all have to be skilled at when they grow up, but we never talked with them about it. We never showed them the pool. We just allowed them to stand outside closed doors and listen to all the splashing. Occasionally, they might catch a glimpse of partially-clothed people going in and out of the door to the pool and maybe they'd find a hidden book on the art of swimming, but when they asked a question about how swimming felt or what it was about, they would be greeted with blank or embarrassed looks. Suddenly, when they turn 18 we would fling open the doors to the swimming pool and they would jump in. Miraculously, some might learn to tread water, but many would drown.

What sorts of things would I suggest that you say to your kids? Here are some examples of things that I tell my colleagues about how to counsel teenagers about sex:

- If you ask teenagers if they have any questions about sex, the answer will invariably be no.
- Avoid jargon.
- Do not immediately assume that you are being understood.
- Avoid lectures. Give them credit for being capable of intelligence, thoughtfulness, and responsibility.
- Do not be afraid to offer your opinions and counsel in a straightforward way. Teenagers will respond to this.
- Do not try to talk to the teenager in the current adolescent vernacular unless this is your usual mode of speaking.

And here are some of the items that I would suggest for the content of such discussions:

- It is always okay to say no, whether you are male or female. Sex should never be used as a test of love. "If you love me, you'll have sex with me" is simply a line, and there are many easy and clever responses to it. (See Sol Gordon's book *Seduction Lines*, listed in appendix I.)

• Not all teenagers are sexually active.
• The decision to begin having intercourse puts a teenager at risk of pregnancy and sexually transmitted disease. These risks can be lessened, but there is nothing as safe as abstinence.
• Sexual fantasies and masturbation are normal.
• Penis and breast size are variable and have no relationship to sexual functioning.
• Sexual fantasies about or experiences with members of the same sex do not necessarily mean that a teenager is homosexual.
• Taking oral contraceptives is ten to twenty-five times as safe as carrying a pregnancy to term.

Now, for all of you parents out there who prefer to avoid this subject altogether and hope for the best, here is a rude surprise for you: Even if you're not talking to your kids at home about sex, they're getting sex education from you anyway. Kids are very perceptive. Every time you touch or don't touch, or blush, or make a fuss when your spouse makes a big public display of affection for you, or snicker at an off-color joke, your kids are practically taking notes. More likely than not, if you can't talk about sex, they are getting the message loud and clear that sex is something secret and dirty. And they certainly may not be interpreting your actions the way you would like to have them interpreted. So why not take control of the situation and talk to them yourself? If you're nervous, *say* you're nervous—they'll know it just by looking at you, but at least it will acknowledge to them that you know that they know that you are. Tell them why you're nervous—probably because your parents didn't like talking to you about such matters.

I know that some of you are still going to ignore my advice, even if I remind you that medical studies indicate that if you talk to your kids about sex, they are *less* likely, not more likely, to engage in intercourse at a young age. That's okay. Maybe you're shy, or you don't believe the studies, or you don't know what to say, or you're afraid your kids will think you foolish. Here's what you do (this is actually how I received the majority of my sex education —and I knew more at age ten than any of my friends): Find a book about sex that you feel is appropriate for your child and contains the sort of things you would like her to know. Leave it on top of your night stand for about a week. I guarantee you, it will be read! I call it Sex Education for the Squeamish.

It stands to reason that if I am urging you to educate your children at home about sex, I am also in favor of sex education in schools. Why? Because such programs can compensate for those of you who are not going to talk to your kids at home. And it can add a lot more information in a much less threatening or sensitive way. Besides, by the time kids reach age ten or twelve, they should know all about "the basic plumbing." What they want to know as teenagers are the answers to such questions as:

- What do I tell my boyfriend when he says, "You don't love me if you won't do it with me"?
- How come everybody I know seems to be having sex but me?
- How do you know if you're homosexual?
- Is birth control dangerous?
- How do you know when you're ready to have sex?

These are the gray areas that may make you particularly nervous. But your kids want to hear the answers to these questions, not only from you, but from other adults they like (such as teachers) and from their peers. Then and only then can they begin to formulate their own ideas about what is right and feasible and ethical for themselves.

Please do not assume that teenagers today are any more knowledgeable than you were when you were growing up. A lot of the same myths are still around. For example, a survey of a thousand teenagers nationwide, conducted by Louis Harris and Associates (*American Teens Speak: Sex, Myths, TV and Birth Control*, 1986) found the following:

Questions Asked of Teenagers	Answer Wrong or Uncertain
A girl usually cannot become pregnant if she has intercourse during her menstrual period (TRUE)	76%
It is possible for a girl to become pregnant even though her male partner's penis did not actually enter her vagina (TRUE)	65%
The time when a girl is most likely to become pregnant is about 2 weeks after her menstrual period begins (TRUE)	59%
A girl has to have an orgasm during intercourse in order to become pregnant (FALSE)	41%
A girl cannot become pregnant if she douches with Coca-Cola after intercourse (FALSE)	28%

A girl cannot become pregnant the first time she has intercourse (FALSE)	20%

You'll notice that I haven't said a word about what you should say to your kids about premarital sex, other than perhaps trying to correct some of their misperceptions. That's because the content of such discussions is entirely up to you. If you believe that your kids shouldn't have sex before marriage, tell them. If you think it's okay for your kids to have sex when they're eighteen or older and involved in a committed relationship, fine. It doesn't matter *what* you say, so long as you say *something* and leave the lines of communication open.

A number of the books and organizations cited in the appendixes might help you with this process. In addition, your church or synagogue will be more than willing to give you information and support. Don't let ignorance or shyness keep you from educating your children about one of the most important aspects of their lives. And remember, even if you don't say a word to your kids, they are still getting powerful messages from you about sex.

SEX EDUCATION AT SCHOOL

As important as parental sex education is, school-based programs are just as important. But, as with parental education, school programs are useful only if they span the continuum from kindergarten through twelfth grade. A one-semester quick-fix program is not going to succeed any more than my father's attempt at the "big lecture" did. Sex ed programs need to be comprehensive in scope. That means teaching not only the biology, but also about pregnancy, STDs, birth control, and *feelings*. Obviously, you are not going to subject a third-grade class to talk of

IUDs and diaphragms—that discussion can wait until they are twelve or thirteen. But you certainly can talk to third-graders about reporting if anyone tries to touch them and that their bodies are their own.

Why sex education remains such a controversy in the United States is a mystery to me, especially given the pervasive influence of television and other media. Why are Americans are so ambivalent, so hysterical about sex? Even the British do a better job of sex education in their schools than we do, and we've always thought of them as repressed and humorless. What I don't understand is why we can't get beyond the controversy. The facts are clear: Sex education programs in schools do not increase or decrease rates of teenage sexual activity. Sex education simply increases kids' knowledge about sex (if it's taught well). End of discussion. Unfortunately, sex ed somehow gets turned into a political issue, not a scientific one, and school boards traditionally run scared of the vocal minority that show up at meetings, declaring that sex education will destroy children's moral values and turn them all into young sexpots.

One reason why sex education is not the panacea it was once thought to be is that many teenagers begin sexual intercourse before they are exposed to a sex education course. A 1984 national survey demonstrated that, of sexually active fifteen-year-olds, only 48 percent of the females and 26 percent of the males had received sex education at school. Even by age eighteen, only 61 percent of the females and 52 percent of the males had taken a course.* Recently the Alan Guttmacher Institute studied state sex education policies in 1988 and made some sur-

* Strasburger, Victor C., ed. "Current Issues in Adolescent Sexuality." *Basic Adolescent Gynecology: An Office Guide*. Baltimore, MD: Urban & Schwarzenberg, 1990.

prising discoveries: Of the nearly $6.3 million spent on sex education by states in 1987–88, $5.1 million was specifically targeted for AIDS education. Nearly one-third of sex ed teachers felt that their biggest obstacle was pressure from parents and school administrators, particularly if they tried to address issues of homosexuality, condoms, and abortion. And while thirty-two states require or encourage instruction about pregnancy prevention, only Delaware and Georgia specifically mandate that the risks and benefits of all contraceptive methods be discussed.

THE ALTERNATIVES TO SEX EDUCATION

At this point, I have probably made a few of you feel a little guilty. Don't worry—you've still got a lot of time to educate your kids about sex and sexuality. And, perhaps the following study might amuse you: In a provocative study entitled "Is There Sex After 40?" (*Psychology Today*, June 1977), 646 college students were asked how often they thought their parents were now having sex. One-fourth of the students did not think their parents had sex anymore, or at best, less than once a year. Half of the students thought the figure was once a month or less. The studies concluded: "Many families head off discussion of sexual matters through a conspiracy of silence. Neither adults nor offspring really want to know what the other is doing. The parents, particularly, may suspect the worst, but they'd rather hope for the best." So you see—you don't want to think about or acknowledge your children's sexuality, and they don't want to think about or acknowledge yours, either!

As a society, we pay a very high price for our teenagers' sexual activity. The United States has the highest rate of teenage pregnancy in the Western world. Over one million teenage pregnancies occur annually in the United

States, resulting in 400,000 abortions and 470,000 live births. One in ten girls becomes pregnant each year, and, at present rates, four in ten will become pregnant while still in their teens. Of teens fifteen years old or younger, more than 30,000 become pregnant annually. These are chilling statistics. We can sit and argue for hours about what the ideal age is for beginning to have sexual intercourse, but no one in his right mind thinks that having a baby at fifteen is a very good idea.

Now, there are a variety of reasons why you may be thinking to yourself, "This section doesn't apply to me." For example, many parents think "it's those poor kids in the inner city that are the problem. My kids would never do this." Wrong. Teenage sexual activity knows no racial or socioeconomic barriers or boundaries. White, middle-class suburban kids are just as likely as poor inner-city kids to be having sexual intercourse at age sixteen. The only difference is that the suburban girl who is upwardly mobile and becomes pregnant is more likely to opt for an abortion than the inner-city teenager. But take the inner-city girl—no matter what color her skin is—to the suburbs, give her a middle-class home and upbringing, and help her to aspire to some future goal like becoming a doctor or lawyer, and she, too, will choose an abortion or adoption over trying to raise a baby herself. Or perhaps you're thinking, "My kids are just eight and ten years old —I don't need to worry about this for a few more years at least." These are crucial years in your child's development. Time spent now, teaching them what "proper values" are, will pay rich dividends when they are adolescents.

Also, as a taxpayer, you need to worry as well. Teen pregnancies cost American taxpayers an estimated $20 billion a year in public funding support. An estimated half of all women who receive AFDC (welfare) payments had teenage pregnancies. In other words, your taxes would actually decrease significantly if we could make a dent in the teenage pregnancy rate.

Identifying At-Risk Teenagers

If I am telling you that you need to worry if you have preteens, how much do you need to worry if you have a fourteen- or fifteen-year-old? In general, approximately 50 percent of high school seniors have engaged in sexual intercourse at least once. Currently, the median age for first sexual intercourse for females in the United States is about sixteen, and for males it is nearly a year younger. But one recent study (Robert W. Blum, *The State of Adolescent Health in Minnesota*, 1989) shows that you may need to begin worrying long before age fifteen or sixteen. More than thirty-six thousand public school students were surveyed by researchers in Minnesota in 1986–87, and they found the following:

- One-third of males and one-fourth of females who have experienced intercourse have done so by age thirteen.
- By twelfth grade, 55 percent of females and 70 percent of males have had intercourse. [Conversely, nearly half of all seventeen- to eighteen-year-old females and nearly one-third of all seventeen- to eighteen-year-old males had never had intercourse. Is the glass half empty or half full?]
- Adolescent sexual intercourse is sporadic: Seventy-five percent of teens report engaging in intercourse either rarely (a few times a year or less) or occasionally (one to four times a month).
- At all ages, metropolitan teenagers are more likely to

have begun having intercourse than their more rural counterparts.

It should go without saying that all teenagers are not created equal, and not all sixteen-year-olds are having sex. What determines whether your teenager is at particular risk for beginning sexual relations early? Interestingly enough, all of the studies point to one major factor: you! Researchers Shirley L. Jessor and Richard Jessor at the University of Colorado did an important study several years ago, reported in *Developmental Psychology* II, 1975. They wanted to know why certain students decide to begin having sex at a young age while others decide to wait. They studied nine hundred high school and college students over four years. Their findings were that the sexually active group: expected and valued achievement less; were more tolerant of differences between themselves and others; were less religious; were more likely to have friends whose views differed from their own parents' views; were more easily influenced by their peers; had more rigid parents; and were more likely to use alcohol and marijuana.

The overall picture here adds up to a teenager who is less close to her parents and therefore less influenced by them, and is more in sync with the peer group. Although it is probably true that religion plays a role, other studies have found that even conservative religious youth can show surprisingly high rates of sexual intercourse: In a 1987 study (reported in *Family Planning Perspectives*, 20(5), 1988) of nearly fifteen hundred "born-again" teenagers, 43 percent were sexually active by age eighteen.

Many theorists like to think of teen sex as a "risk-taking behavior" that accompanies drug use. But the connection here may be that drugs such as alcohol and marijuana lower inhibitions against having sex. I prefer to look at early sexual activity in the context of the changing American family. Adolescents have a special need for closeness, and if that need is not being met at home, they may seek alternative ways of fulfilling it. Many studies have implicated family instability as an important factor in early teenage sexual intercourse and pregnancy. In addition, several studies have found that a teenager's unhappiness at home, or her feelings of alienation from her mother, in particular, are associated with an earlier age at first intercourse and with having multiple partners. Rates of sexual intercourse are also increased among teens whose mothers had a teenage pregnancy themselves, or were married young.

Most parents would like to believe that religion and high self-esteem protect against early sex, and they do to some extent, but more important is academic and school success. The 1986 Harris Report also found that sexual intercourse was highest among teens with poor school grades and teens whose parents were not college graduates. And a recent large national study by Allan Abrahamse, Peter Morrison, and Linda Waite (*Family Planning Perspectives* 20, 1988) of more than thirteen thousand high-school sophomores found that just three factors could explain teenagers' willingness to have children outside of marriage: socioeconomic level, academic ability, and being raised in a single-parent household.

What role does that old adolescent bugaboo, peer pressure, play in teenage sexual activity? Many teenagers think that everyone is having intercourse except them. Teens *do* report social pressure and peer pressure as two key reasons for their beginning sexual intercourse early, but this could represent rationalization more than anything else. In a study by Robert Coles and Geoffrey Stokes (*Sex and the American Teenager*, Harper & Row, 1985), 78 percent of the virgins thought their friends were virgins as well, while 72 percent of the nonvirgins thought their friends were similarly experienced. That would confirm the "birds of a feather" theory of peer groups rather than the "one evil, corrupting peer group" theory. Certainly, the media constitute their own, unique source of social and peer pressure, and we'll devote an entire chapter to looking at how the media may be influencing your child's behavior.

One of the most interesting items to come out of several recent surveys is that the old double standard seems to be alive and well in America. Guys are expected to have sex as soon as they can possibly arrange it, but girls are still expected to remain chaste. At every age there is a large discrepancy between the number of males and females who have had sex. In addition, in the few studies that have looked at numbers of sexual partners, guys win easily. Most girls who have engaged in sexual intercourse have only had one partner *and* felt "in love" with or committed to that partner. (Note: Although most female teenagers would seem to subscribe to the adult philosophy that sexual intercourse should occur only in the context of a mature, loving, committed relationship, their concept of being "in love" does not coincide with adults' version. In one survey, 52 percent of all the teenagers believed that they had been in love by age thirteen, and 84 percent by age eighteen!) Many guys, on the other hand, will have sex with anything that moves and breathes. I know you're thinking that I am just perpetuating the same old myths about guys being perpetually horny and girls belonging up on a pedestal. But the data don't lie. And the biological facts are incontrovertible: It is the teenage girl who becomes pregnant *and* who is at greatest risk for acquiring an STD, since male-to-female transmission of STDs is far more efficient than vice versa. So, in the long run, teenage girls seem to behave more responsibly than guys yet suffer far more from the consequences of their sexual activity. So, yes, I must confess that I do have more sympathy for them.

Despite the perception that "everyone is doing it," teenagers have begun to display their own brand of conservatism about sex. In the same study mentioned above, half of the females wanted to be virgins at marriage; and a Baltimore study of thirty-five hundred junior and senior high school students found that 32 percent of the males and 39 percent of the females actually thought that premarital sex was wrong.

What the Data Mean

As a parent, the best way for you to interpret all this data is simply to realize that a lot of teenagers are having sex—although certainly not all teenagers. And if you want to try to prevent your child from having sex at age fourteen, the place to begin is in your own family, *not* in worrying about some quick-fix, "just say no," self-esteem–raising program in school. Even if your family does not fit the high-risk profile, your teenager could still be sexually active without your knowing about it. Do not assume that you are safe because your family is intact and you feel that the lines of communication are open. Conversely, do not panic because you are a single parent. I see many teenagers who are fifteen, sixteen, and seventeen and are not yet sexually active and enjoy very close relationships with both of their divorced parents. These teenagers are rarely happy that their parents have split up, but they do not feel trapped by it either. Sometimes the fact of divorce can open new lines of communication and build new sensitivities for all concerned.

When I see a teenager in my office, what increases my suspicion that he is having sex? "Macho males" always arouse my suspicion, because I know that if they are having intercourse, they may be pressuring their partners to have sex and undoubtedly are leaving the burden of contraception up to the girls. Susan M. Barbieri, an *Orlando Sentinel* reporter, was asked to interview a group of teenagers for a story. As she reported (May 17, 1992):

> Things were going well—until the 14-year-old boys in the group went into Macho Mode and began telling jokes.
> "How many men does it take to scrub a floor? . . . None. That's women's work," said one boy. Added another: "How do you get a dishwasher to work? . . . Slap her."
> . . . What kind of men will they become? At one end of the spectrum, perhaps they will become men who simply lack respect for women. (Future members of the Senate Judiciary Committee?) At the other end of the continuum, perhaps they will become men who think it's OK to force themselves on women. (Future pro boxers?)

Where are such attitudes learned? Probably at home. Definitely in the media. And probably in the teenager's peer group as well. How you and your spouse respond to sexist jokes at home, how you treat each other, how you react to sexism portrayed on television and in the movies —all of this helps to shape the next generation's sense of what maleness and femaleness are all about. (The same holds true for racism.) A stern "That's not very funny, and I don't want to hear you talking like that again" after a sexist joke told by your ten-year-old boy can go far toward teaching him proper respect for the opposite sex.

If a teenage girl has a steady boyfriend who is two or more years older than she is, that is almost a guarantee that they are having intercourse. Certainly, there is a strong element of pressure in many such relationships. And many of the young girls I treat do not seem to be enjoying intercourse very much—it's simply their way of keeping their boyfriend.

But the only way for me to know, for 100 percent sure, if a teenager is having sex is to ask him. And that goes for you, too. If you want to know what your teenager is up to, *ask!* Some teenagers may resent that kind of intrusion into their personal lives. Others, however, may feel close enough to their mothers, in particular, to acknowledge that they are having sex, or they are thinking about having sex with a new boyfriend or girlfriend. So again, I can't give you a one-line piece of advice that will cover all families and all situations. I can tell you how I ask teenagers in my office about their sexual activities. Some kids I can ask directly: "Are you having sex with anyone?" Others seem more shy or reticent, so I begin by discussing their friends: "Are any of your friends pregnant?" "Have any of your friends gotten any girls pregnant?" "Are any of your friends having sex?" That line of questioning gives me an entrée into the teenager's thoughts on the subject, and we proceed from there. Of course, you shouldn't be questioning your teenager about sex unless you're prepared to hear an answer you might not like.

That's where contraception comes in. Again let me remind you: If your teenage son impregnates a girl, and particularly if your teenage daughter becomes pregnant, they can kiss their adolescence good-bye. If it's your daughter, she can probably kiss her economic future good-bye, as well as her husband, should she decide to marry the father of the baby. Nearly 70 percent of pregnant teens drop out of school, and many never obtain their high school degree. A young woman without a high school degree and with a small infant to care for has a minuscule chance of achieving economic independence. Sure, a few brave kids make it through to college, or law school, or medical school, but they are the rare exceptions.

If teenagers marry because of a pregnancy, they have a 50 percent chance of being divorced within two years. Teenage pregnancy is a societal disaster. It costs us billions of dollars a year, it fosters a huge and disruptive debate about contraception and abortion, and it wrecks lives and families.

Here is a startling bit of scientific data: The United States has the highest teenage pregnancy rate in the Western world *despite the fact that American teenagers are no more sexually active than their European counterparts.* In fact, they are considerably *less* sexually active than Swedish teenagers, yet our rate of teenage pregnancy is two to ten times as high as that of any other Western nation. The reason for this is actually surprisingly simple: Americans' attitude toward sex and birth control, which people in other countries and cultures simply don't have.

Take a look around you. In our culture, nearly every billboard, TV show, and best-selling novel says, "Have sex. It's fun. It's sexy. And it's got no risks. Besides, everyone else is doing it." In American society, we use sex to sell everything from cars to shampoo to hotel rooms, yet when our children respond to these cues and begin having sex at age thirteen or fourteen, we suddenly become puritanical and blame them for their lewd and lascivious behavior. Where did they learn such things, we mutter to ourselves. Well, open your eyes—they learned from us! At the same time that we manufacture all of these enticing cues about sex, we refuse to educate our children about sex, either at home or at school, and we become positively apoplectic at the idea of offering them birth control.

The bottom line is, it's up to us. We're the generation who wanted to change the world. Here is our golden opportunity. Except that, rather than changing the arms race or the American political process, we have to look a little closer to home: at our children. For their sake, and yours, *talk* to them about sex. Not one big lecture; rather, create an air of being an approachable parent, willing to discuss anything, no matter how shocking it might be or how strenuously you may object. Break the generational silence about sex and sexuality. Because if you don't, you can be sure that their friends and the media will. Prevention of early sexual activity starts with you!

TEENAGE SEX: THE CONTROVERSIAL AREAS

Let's finish up by talking some more about the nitty-gritty of adolescent sex, so that you'll know what to say to your kids if it turns out that the answer to the big question is yes. Here I will not be speaking to you as a "pro-choicer" or a "pro-lifer," but rather as a pediatrician who treats teenagers and would like to see them remain healthy. This is a scientific issue and a health issue. It is *not*, and should not be, a political hot potato. We know a lot about how to prevent teen pregnancies, but we seem to be tripping over our own feet.

Let's back up just a little and discuss how adolescents actually use *birth control*. Teenagers are not good contraceptors. Many surveys have found that perhaps only one-third of teenage females use contraception at first intercourse, with age being the most significant predictor of use. Even after having had a sexual relationship for several weeks or months, only 50 percent of teenagers use birth control. At first intercourse, condoms are the most frequently used method. After a while the pill becomes the method of choice.

Many studies document that age is the single most important factor in who uses birth control and who doesn't —in other words, teenagers eventually mature. They begin to understand and appreciate the very real risks associated with sexual activity.

After age, the most important predictors of contraceptive use are similar to the predictors of early sexual activity: having an intact family, educational level of the teenager's mother, social class, and neighborhood quality —in other words, "upward mobility." Poor inner-city teenagers who have nothing to aspire to are less likely to use birth control than middle-class suburban teenagers who plan to go to college and graduate school. The issue is not skin color but their view of their future and probably their sophistication in being able to deal with a difficult medical system.

One problem that we physicians face in treating adolescents is that there is no one ideal form of birth control. Every method has its advantages and disadvantages. For example, from a psychological point of view the pill is the ideal birth control for teenagers. It separates the act of contracepting from the act of having sex, and that's important for female teenagers, many of whom feel somewhat guilty about planning to have sex. The pill allows them to hold on to their romantic "I'm in love and I'm being swept away" fantasies. Also, when taken as directed, the pill is 99.7 percent effective in preventing pregnancy. No other birth control method approaches that degree of protection. On the other hand, a package of pills costs ten to fifteen dollars a month; you have to make an appointment with a physician to get a prescription, and that requires having a pelvic exam done as well; it's easy for your mother to discover them in your purse or bureau drawer; they do occasionally have some unpleasant side effects (breakthrough bleeding, for example); and—perhaps most important in this era of AIDS—they offer *no* protection against STDs.

These days many physicians would prefer to see teen-

agers use condoms. Condoms are cheap and readily available (although you've got to work up enough nerve to
buy them in public), and they prevent STDs, including
the transmission of HIV. Unfortunately, girls are shy
about buying them, guys don't like to use them, and they
are only about 90 to 95 percent effective in preventing
pregnancy, because people don't use them properly or
they tear. Despite all of the emphasis on "safe sex" these
days, condoms are not a very popular form of birth control
among teenagers, although many teens will *say* that they
use them, because they know it's the right thing to say or
it's what we health professionals want to hear. Another
problem is that even people who use them don't use them
all the time. A survey of nearly two thousand Massachu-
setts teens found that the use of condoms has increased
from 2 percent to 19 percent in the past two years, but 19
percent is still not a very reassuring figure, and intensive
"safe sex" campaigns in San Francisco and in Denmark
have failed to increase condom use among adolescents.
Clearly, less than a majority of sexually active teenagers
use condoms all the time, and high-risk teens (those who
have multiple sexual partners or are drug users) are the
least likely to use them.

In the sixties and early seventies intrauterine devices
(IUDs) were touted as the ideal form of contraception for
teenagers: You could just have one inserted and be protected for the next few years. Unfortunately, the medical
risks weren't appreciated at the time: an increased risk of
pelvic inflammatory disease and sterility. Now, even
though IUDs are considerably safer and making a bit of a
comeback, they are still not recommended for women
under age twenty-five or for women whose childbearing
has not yet been completed. The 1990s version of an IUD
is called Norplant: six small matchsticks that are implanted
underneath the skin of the arm rather than being inserted

into the uterus. From the early studies, Norplant seems to be both safe and effective, but it costs five hundred to seven hundred dollars and involves minor surgery, and therefore is not likely to be popular with teenagers.

Finally, the diaphragm is a very safe and reliable form of birth control, but teenagers don't like to use it. It is more appropriate for the college-age young woman who is better motivated about planning to contracept and is less shy about touching herself in intimate places. Diaphragms are messy and require insertion no more than an hour before having sex. They offer some protection against STDs but are only about 90 to 95 percent effective in preventing pregnancy.

One very popular method of birth control among teenagers, which doesn't work, is withdrawal. It takes more self-control than many adolescent males are capable of, some sperm inevitably leaks out of the penis before orgasm, and the risk of pregnancy is very high. Likewise, periodic abstinence is beyond the capabilities of most adolescents, so the rhythm method is out (and even more difficult are versions of rhythm that call for measuring the woman's basal body temperature, testing cervical mucus, and the like).

It is sad that one million teenage pregnancies a year during the past decade have not been sufficient to interest people in comprehensive sex education programs. It has taken the threat of **AIDS** to do it. AIDS *is* a legitimate threat to your child's health and life. Let's talk a little about what we know about AIDS and what you should be saying to your kids about it.

AIDS was first reported in the United States in 1981 and now constitutes one of the most urgent public health crises in the history of American medicine. The Human

Immunodeficiency Virus (HIV) has been isolated from semen, cervical secretions, blood, urine, amniotic fluid, breast milk, saliva, and tears in patients with AIDS, although these fluids vary considerably in how contagious they are. HIV eventually cripples the host's immune system, paving the way for opportunistic infections, cancer, and autoimmune disorders. Currently, about one million people are infected with the virus in the United States, and by the end of 1991 more than two hundred thousand cases of AIDS had been reported.

Although barely 2 percent of AIDS cases have occurred in thirteen- to twenty-one-year-olds—approximately two thousand cases—there is an increasing realization that many young adults were first infected with HIV during adolescence. This is because full-blown AIDS may take as long as ten to fourteen years to develop from the time of first infection. Twenty percent of all AIDS cases are diagnosed in twenty- to twenty-nine-year-olds, and the incubation period for AIDS among homosexual and bisexual men is an estimated eleven years. But actual AIDS cases probably represent the tip of the iceberg: For every case, an estimated three to five people have AIDS-related complex (ARC) and another fifty to a hundred people are infected with HIV but are asymptomatic. If these estimates are correct, the United States will be faced with one to two million cases of AIDS in the near future.

Exactly how many adolescents are infected with HIV is still unclear, but we know that certain groups of adolescents are at high risk: As many as one in a hundred adolescents in endemic areas like New York and San Francisco are HIV-positive. Among homeless and runaway youth in New York City, the rate of infection with HIV was 7 percent in one study of fifteen hundred teenagers and 16 percent in eighteen- to twenty-year-olds. And a recent survey of more than sixteen thousand college students at nineteen universities throughout the United States found an overall prevalence of one in five hundred students infected. All were over eighteen years old, nearly two-thirds were over twenty-four years old, and all but two were men.

Among the first twelve hundred AIDS cases diagnosed in thirteen- to twenty-one-year-olds, 70 percent were secondary to homosexual or bisexual transmission. However, adolescent females may be at particular risk from heterosexual sex, unlike their male or adult counterparts. In New York City, half of the adolescent cases could be attributed to heterosexual sex—twice the percentage of adult cases.

Any activity that can disrupt normal skin, mucous membranes, or blood barriers can lead to infection. This includes intravenous drug use with contaminated needles, transfusion with infected blood products, or contact of vaginal or rectal mucosa with infected bodily fluids.

At present, there is no cure for AIDS. Since AIDS is a fatal disease, prevention is crucial. Among high-risk populations, homosexual men need to avoid receptive anal intercourse and use condoms. Intravenous drug users must avoid sharing needles. Women whose sexual partners are intravenous drug users or bisexual are also at high risk. And all women should be aware of the fact that male-to-female transmission of the virus appears to be far more efficient than vice versa.

What constitutes "safe sex"? Obviously, no sex at all is safest. But at some point in your lives that sort of advice becomes impractical. Therefore, physicians routinely counsel:

• Reduction in number of sexual partners
• Emphasis on permanent mutual monogamy

- Use of condoms
- Avoidance of anal intercourse

However, we may be seriously deceiving ourselves that there is such a thing as "safe sex." The idea that you should "know your partner" seems particularly foolish. Do those of you who are single or divorced feel confident enough to question your partners about previous sexual activities? Do you think they will give you an honest answer, or even know the sexual histories of *their* previous partners? And if adults don't feel comfortable trying to elicit this sort of history, do you really think that teenagers stand a chance?

Teenagers' knowledge about AIDS seems to be increasing, but there continues to be a need for thoughtful school-based education programs that will deal with harmful attitudes as well as lack of knowledge. For example, nearly half of teenagers in one Wisconsin survey reported that homosexuals and intravenous drug users with AIDS were simply "getting what they deserve."

As with sex education in general, education about AIDS and HIV can be effective but should *never* involve so-called scare tactics. There is *no* evidence that teenagers can be dissuaded from initiating sexual intercourse by the threat of AIDS, or that scare tactics will even prevent teenagers from engaging in high-risk activities. Indeed, as we have seen, normal adolescent psychology would seem to indicate the exact opposite: Most teenagers think, "It could never happen to me." What we may be doing when we employ such tactics is to cheapen or diminish the positive aspects of human sex. Many professionals worry that this generation will grow up fearing sex or associating sex with death. *Please, do not,* under any circumstances, *try to use AIDS to scare your kids away from having sex at a young age.*

What are the chances that your child will ever develop

AIDS? Slight, certainly—although the odds are increasing all the time. But the risks are real, even for heterosexuals. For the first time in the history of the antibiotic era, a sexual encounter can literally kill.

So what should you be telling your child? I would suggest placing HIV and AIDS in the context of sexually transmitted diseases. HIV is a virus that is most often acquired through sexual intercourse. The risk of acquiring HIV is relatively small, but it is one more item that must be put into the equation in thinking about when and with whom to begin having sexual relations. You might admit that, had HIV been around when you were sixteen, you would have been much more cautious about embarking on a sexual relationship. It is certainly fair to tell your kids, if they should ask, that yes, you and your spouse did have sex before marriage, but, given the current risk of HIV and AIDS, you probably wouldn't if you had things to do over again. Some teenagers may accuse their parents of being hypocritical and "changing the rules," but the rules *have* been changed, and not by any of us. Kids are always fond of telling their parents, "Times are different. Things have changed. We have to do things differently from when you were growing up." Here is your opportunity to turn the tables and use this argument to your advantage. And, in this particular case, turnabout *is* fair play (and good medicine).

In the context of HIV as an STD, I tell all of my patients that having sex will put them at risk. The risk may be small, or it may seem worth taking. One way for them to minimize the risk is to wait to have sex until they are older. There is a good biological reason for this: The cervix of an adolescent is less resistant to infection than the cervix of an older woman, for example. Older teenagers are also far more likely to use effective means of birth control. I also tell my patients about "safe sex," particularly the part about not having more than one sexual partner. It is simply the law of probability: The more people you have sex with, the greater the chance that you will acquire an STD. It's just like playing the lottery. Most kids will understand that kind of reasoning.

❑   ❑   ❑

Finally, a few words about abortion—the biggest area of controversy of all.

❑

NANCY: Nancy W. is an articulate, attractive fifteen-year-old who comes to see me because she has been having abdominal pains and vomiting for the past week. I ask her if there's a possibility that she could be pregnant, and she says yes. Her urine pregnancy test is positive, and she is approximately eight weeks pregnant, by my exam. Nancy is extremely upset and tearful and asks me to inform her mother, which I do. Then I ask them to return the following day to discuss the situation further.

The next morning, both of Nancy's parents accompany her to my office. Nancy is an A student who wants to go to either Harvard or MIT and eventually on to medical school. Her boyfriend, an eighteen-year-old Hispanic male, is a high school dropout, currently living with friends. Mr. W. wants to file charges against him for statutory rape and wants Nancy to have an abortion. Mrs. W. also thinks an abortion would be a good idea but is willing to support Nancy in whichever decision she makes, although she would not be able to help with childrearing.

When I talk to Nancy alone, she says that she is very confused: "Everyone in my family is telling me what to do; they all tell me that I'm too young to even know what's best for me." She has always thought that abor-

tions were "wrong," although now she is not so sure. She thinks she could raise a baby and still make it to college, although not Harvard or MIT, and probably not medical school afterward. She says she is "too young to be a mother," but "I got myself into this, and I should pay the price." I ask her if that is fair, either to herself or to her baby, should she continue the pregnancy. She refuses to even consider giving the baby up for adoption.

With Nancy and her parents present, I explain the pros and cons of her having an abortion, giving the baby up for adoption, or keeping the baby. The next day, Nancy returns with her boyfriend. He is tattooed to his elbows. Although they hold hands, he does not seem very affectionate toward Nancy, nor is he happy with this entire situation. When asked directly, he says that he will go along with whatever option Nancy chooses. But clearly the prospect of being a teenage father does not excite him.

I ask Nancy what she is thinking, and she says she still doesn't know what to do. I offer to meet with her again, whenever she needs to talk with someone. She thanks me and leaves the office, walking very slowly. Two weeks later she calls to tell me that she has had an abortion.

❑

There is an incredible amount of misinformation about abortion out there, so let's start by setting the record straight. First, no one in his right mind thinks that abortions are a great idea. Even pro-choice people thoroughly dislike the idea of abortion. So the term "pro-life" is really a kind of Orwellian double speak. We're *all* pro-life, aren't we?

Next, a first-trimester abortion is one of the safest surgical procedures performed. There is virtually no risk of death from a first-trimester abortion, and very little risk of major complications. In fact, having a first-trimester abortion is five to ten times as safe as carrying a pregnancy to term. And, make no mistake about it, girls and women did die in back alleys before the 1973 *Roe* v. *Wade* decision.

Third, having a baby as a teenager can be a real life sentence, with parole possible only after eighteen years. And it can be a life sentence for the baby as well—condemned to being raised in poverty, with perhaps an increased risk of being abused, by a mother who is still a child herself. It is not a very pretty picture either.

It would be ideal if we could just ask all the pregnant teenagers who don't want to keep their pregnancies to give up their babies for adoption. Everyone agrees that of the three options—delivery, abortion, adoption—adoption is by far the best. But less than 5 percent of teenage girls are willing to give up their babies for adoption. My wife and I were fortunate enough to benefit from the gift of one of them, a very strong-willed sixteen-year-old who wanted to go on to college and graduate school and wanted "something better" for her baby than what she thought she could give. You will not find a more eager fan of adoption than yours truly. But, as an adolescent medicine specialist, I have to tell you that it's just not in the cards for most teenagers. Normal adolescent psychology prevents 95 percent of teenage girls from giving up their babies; they think about themselves and how they will give this baby all the love they never had, rather than about the baby's best interests. Young teenagers also have wildly unrealistic notions about what it means to have a baby, what it costs and how much time and energy are involved. So although adoption is a noble compromise, it is also, sadly, an impractical one.

So here's the bottom line: We are trapping our teenagers in the cross-fire between antiabortion and proabortion groups. If we took all of the time and energy and money that the different factions have devoted to this issue and applied it instead to preventing teenage pregnancy, we could cut the teenage pregnancy rate in half. But no, we adults have to exercise our "moral consciences," even if we hurt our own children in the process. Do I sound angry? I am. Clearly, this is an emotional debate and one that will never be solved by logic or science or even the law. So why not compromise? Here is what I suggest: The "pro-life" people should concede that first-trimester abortions are acceptable, and the "pro-choice" people should concede that second-trimester and third-trimester abortions are unacceptable, except in the case of medical risk to the woman. I can already hear both sides howling in protest—which is precisely why this is such a good compromise! Each side has to give up something that is extremely important to it. The "pro-lifers" would be acknowledging the "pro-choice" view that abortion is an acceptable alternative to pregnancy, and the "pro-choicers" would be validating the "pro-life" concern that at some point the fetus takes on a life of its own. Only if we compromise on this issue—arbitrarily, I admit—can we get on with our lives and stop wasting valuable time and energy on this issue.

I make this proposal as someone who is a passionate advocate for teenagers, recognizing full well that they might be harmed by it: After all, teenagers have a disproportionate number of second-trimester abortions (because they deny the fact that they could be pregnant until it's too late). But I would be willing to make this sacrifice so that we can have some peace on this issue. And then we can begin looking at the crucial issues, such as how to prevent teenagers from becoming sexually active at too young an age, and how we can keep those who do from experiencing the catastrophe of teen pregnancy or sexually transmitted disease.

❑ ❑ ❑

I started this chapter with the case histories of Marti, Bennett, and Dana—all typical teenagers with well-meaning but misguided parents. It's not easy raising a teenager in the 1990s, and sex is probably the single most anxiety-producing aspect of modern adolescence. But you *must* deal with it—calmly, intelligently, and effectively. Otherwise, you will be doing what most of our parents did with us: burying their heads in the sand and hoping for the best. Without your guidance, your kids may still turn out fine, but the odds are tremendously improved if you become part of the solution, not part of the problem. Talk to your kids, become strong advocates of comprehensive sex education in school, seek help from your pediatrician or family physician. But—to use a good sixties expression—do not stand idly by.

Chapter 4

Getting Your Kids to "Just Say No" to Drugs in the 90s When You "Just Said Yes" to Drugs in the 60s

❏

Slogans that teach young people to 'Say no' to drugs or sex have a nice ring to them. But . . . they are as effective in prevention of adolescent pregnancy and drug abuse as the saying 'Have a nice day' is in preventing clinical depression.

—MICHAEL CARRERA, Ed.D., testifying at the Presidential Commission on AIDS

Talkin' 'bout my g-g-g-generation . . . Remember that "harmless little tickle"? That's what John Lennon said about marijuana. How about "Tune in, turn on, drop out"? That was Timothy Leary on using LSD. Recognize "One pill makes you larger, the other makes you small"? It's a line from Jefferson Airplane's hit "White Rabbit." What all of these items have in common is that they are representative of the mainstream drug culture of the

1960s, back when we were growing up. If you grew up within five years on either side of that time period and you *didn't* smoke marijuana, you were like in the minority, man.

So, here again, we as parents are going to have a slightly more difficult time selling "just say no" to our kids, when they know *we* didn't "just say no." Many of us just said yes, sometimes frequently, and with great relish. After all, drugs were one of the primary symbols of our generation, and we were damned proud of it. We were radical, countercultural, far-out. We were breaking down the doors of perception. We were *groovy.*

Well, we're not so groovy anymore. In fact, we now tend to be somewhat conservative and strait-laced about drugs, perhaps even more so because we used them. Have we changed, or have drugs changed, or both?

The answer is both.

❏

RICK: Rick is a seventeen-year-old whose parents requested an evaluation for his "acting out" behavior. A senior in high school, Rick had been a straight-A student in a special college preparatory track until six months ago, when his grades began to deteriorate. He has always been surrounded by friends and been an excellent athlete. Now, he has been extremely disagreeable at home, verbally abusive to both parents, and refusing to obey rules set by them. Recently he had received two tickets for moving violations. Although he was forbidden to use the car, Rick took the keys from his mother's pocketbook, had an extra set made, and used the car anyway. His parents also state that Rick is beginning to associate with a new set of friends who are "into drugs."

Rick's father is a successful businessman who has al-

ways had high expectations for his son but has not had much free time to spend with him. He is also very strict and inflexible in dealing with Rick. He is interested in what he calls a "tough love" approach, which to him means tossing Rick out of the house until he "cleans up his act." Rick's mother frequently has to function as an intermediary between father and son.

I ask to talk with Rick alone. He is tall, muscular, handsome, and extremely bright. He thinks his parents are being "overly paranoid" and that they "have at least as many problems as I do . . . maybe more." When asked about his drug use, Rick states that he uses alcohol and marijuana regularly and "can handle them." He is unsure of what he wants to do in life. "I'll probably go to college and take a look around, but I don't want to be stuck trying to make the big bucks like my father."

❏

Some excellent research indicates that teenage drug use may represent a time-limited pattern of behavior that eventually is either abandoned or lessens in adulthood. In one study, a group of teenagers in 1969 were followed and restudied in 1981, when they were in their mid- to late twenties. More than half of those who were problem drinkers as teenagers no longer were as adults. Nearly half of the women and more than a quarter of the men had stopped using marijuana. Apparently, time is an important and unappreciated ally in combating teenage drug abuse. The important message here is that if we can't completely prevent drug use from the outset, then perhaps the trick is to make sure that teenagers survive long enough to outgrow drugs.

Here is the truthful and appropriate answer to your

child's inevitable question about did you and your spouse use drugs: Times *have* changed, and we now know far more about certain drugs than we did in the 1960s— enough so that now we can unequivocally say, "Don't do as I did; do as I say." Yes, we made a mistake in believing that marijuana was "a harmless tickle." It's not. It's a dangerous drug. So are LSD and cocaine and amphetamines (which most of us would have acknowledged even back in the sixties).

But please, do not get trapped into the "just say no" mentality. Yes, we should remain steadfast in insisting that drug use is bad and kids should not use drugs. But the idea that we can actually accomplish drug prevention by simple sloganeering is just plain foolish. "Just say no," in its simplest form, represents the typical American desire for a quick-fix solution to a complex problem. Getting kids to stay away from drugs involves teaching them how to resist pressure as well as providing them with safe, satisfying alternatives. "The Quack Epidemic," a commentary in the *New Republic* (November 1988), lamented the lack of creative solutions to the drug problem in America:

Can a truly honest message about drugs be driven home without perversely encouraging drug experimentation? We don't know—and that's really our point. For all the money being spent on drug education, there's been very little solid inquiry into what sort of education works. The Nancy Reagan "just say no" campaign? The souped-up, sophisticated "impact" ads (you know, the ones with the egg and the frying pan and the voiceover that says, "This is your brain, this is drugs, and this is your brain on drugs")? Videotapes of the government-invented rock group called The Jets doing their smash hit, "Be Smart! Don't Start"? There's no telling. Our guess, and our hope, is that, when the results are in, the winning formula will be much like the formula that has cut cigarette use sharply: give people accurate information about the risks and trust them.

Interestingly, there are important parallels between teen sex and teen drug use in the United States—similar causes, and a similar hysteria and hypocrisy about how to deal with them. The good news is that the so-called war on drugs seems to be having some measurable impact on kids. The bad news is that we're targeting the wrong drugs! Let's take an in-depth look at who's using what and why, and then at what realistically we can do to prevent teenagers from even experimenting with drugs.

THE DRUGS

The two most important drugs that you need to worry about are nicotine and alcohol—not cocaine, not heroin, not uppers or downers or anabolic steroids. By far, cigarettes and alcohol pose the greatest danger to you and your children. Although the use of cocaine and marijuana has consistently fallen among teenagers during the past decade, the use of cigarettes and alcohol has not. Between 60 and 100 million Americans currently use alcohol and cigarettes, the two legal psychoactive drugs. By comparison, there are less than 5 percent as many users of heroin or cocaine, the two most dangerous illicit drugs.

Cigarettes

In a report issued in February 1991, the Centers for Disease Control announced a record number of deaths from smoking in the United States: 434,000 in 1988, an 11 percent increase since 1985. The annual cost to the American public is over $50 billion. In addition, the U.S. Government continues to underwrite tobacco farmers to the tune of over $500 million a year. *Smoking is the leading cause of preventable deaths in the United States.* Each year approximately one million teenagers begin smoking—approximately three thousand teenagers each day! Currently, about 20 percent of high school seniors smoke regularly, and nearly 30 percent have used cigarettes in the past thirty days. Smokers who begin before the age of fifteen have rates of cancer that are nineteen times as high as those of nonsmokers. Nicotine is one of the most highly addictive drugs known: All it takes to get hooked is completely smoking three cigarettes. Significantly, only 10 to 15 percent of current smokers began smoking after age nineteen. If we can just get teenagers through their adolescence, we probably have protected them for the rest of their lives.

Why do kids start smoking? Their peer group is an important factor. So are the media (as we'll discuss in chapter 5). But you are the most important determining factor in whether your children smoke. If Dad smokes, teenage son is more likely to smoke. If Mom smokes, teenage daughter is more likely to smoke. And if both parents smoke, the risk of their children's smoking is even higher —in fact, children are twice as likely to smoke if their parents smoke. This represents classic role-modeling behavior. If you smoke, or even if you have a lenient or tolerant attitude toward others' smoking, your kids are more likely to get the idea that smoking is okay. In our heyday, we *were* more tolerant of smokers. Although the Surgeon General's Report in 1956 fired the first salvo against tobacco, it really took another decade before all of the risks of primary smoking were delineated (lung cancer, heart disease, etc.), and not until the past few years has secondary, or passive, smoking been found to be hazardous as well. According to the American Academy of Pediatrics, if everyone in the United States who currently smokes quit today, there would be 90 percent less lung cancer, 50 percent less bladder cancer, 33 percent less heart disease, and 22 percent fewer low-birth-weight babies.

Because we grew up in the fifties, sixties, and early seventies, some of us may still be "amused" by such teenage antics as trying to smoke a cigarette and inhaling it incorrectly or becoming nauseated. Don't be. Your children need a strong and consistent message from you that cigarettes are bad news and nicotine is a highly addictive drug. You can't control everything your teenager does, but if the message about cigarettes was loud and clear throughout his childhood, he is going to have to wrestle with it before he gets addicted to cigarettes. Because of their normal feelings of invincibility, teenagers think they can beat the odds, but they can't: Seventy-five percent of daily teenage smokers are still smoking five to seven years later, but only 5 percent *thought* that they would continue to smoke. (On the other hand, I have seen a new generation of kids whose parents smoke and who are completely turned off to smoking. Either these kids are responding to the news about harmful health consequences and are worried about their parents, or their parents have succeeded in convincing them that they became addicted against their will. I was seven years old when the first Surgeon General's report on smoking was issued, and my mother used to smoke unfiltered Chesterfield cigarettes. When she tried to light up at the dining-room table, I used to shoot her lighted matches out with my water pistol, because I was convinced that she was going to die if she continued smoking. She stopped!)

According to a recent pamphlet published by the American Academy of Pediatrics, here are the main messages that you need to give to your children:

1. Smoking is unattractive.
2. Smoking is unhealthy.
3. Tobacco is a killer.
4. Chewing tobacco and smoking tobacco are also harmful.
5. Smoking is addictive.
6. Smoking is expensive.

I would add a seventh message:

7. *Smoking will not be tolerated in this household!*

On the other hand, do not for one moment think that you are going to dissuade your teenager from smoking by telling her that it might give her lung cancer thirty or forty years from now. Teenagers have a difficult time thinking beyond tomorrow, much less next year, and asking them to envision their own adulthood or death simply defies normal adolescent psychology. Instead, it may be worthwhile to appeal to their vanity. Smoking causes bad breath, stained teeth, and facial wrinkles. It puts holes in their expensive designer clothing and makes them smell bad. According to an American Cancer Society survey, more than two-thirds of teenagers aged twelve to seventeen said that they would not want to date someone who smoked. If your children have any athletic aspirations, you can tell them that smoking reduces the amount of oxygen their bloodstream can carry, so that they would not be able to run as well as a nonsmoker.

Even if you believe the foolish propaganda of the American Tobacco Institute that the link between cigarettes and cancer has not been proven, consider this fact: Cigarettes are perhaps the single most important "gateway drug." Once a teenager gets hooked on nicotine, there is a greater chance that he will go on to try other drugs: marijuana, cocaine, amphetamines. There is simply no excuse for our society to tolerate smoking any longer—it makes our health insurance premiums higher, our hospital costs higher, and the risk to ourselves and our loved ones higher (thanks to passive smoking, even if we don't smoke ourselves). Of course, stronger laws against selling cigarettes to minors and banning cigarette vending machines in places where youngsters have access to them would help as well. But, most of all, children need to be taught from the earliest possible age that cigarettes are a harmful drug and an addictive habit.

Alcohol

Dear Abby*: Our oldest son, "John," is going to his first prom. He is 16½ years old and a junior in high school.

John and three other couples planned to rent a hotel room for a post-prom party, and, of course, drink beer. I suggested to my husband that we should have the kids back to our house for a post-prom party. No. 1: I won't have to worry all night about John and his friends being out all night drinking. No. 2: We live five miles from the school where the prom will be held. No. 3: It won't cost us a cent because the kids will pay for their own beer and snacks.

I could keep all of the car keys so no one would have to drive. Also, I could give them all coffee in the morning before they leave. Well, my husband went nuts! He says I am encouraging the kids to drink. I tried to explain that this was a special occasion, and they are going to drink anyway. He thinks I am 100 percent wrong in suggesting they come here, and I think I am 100 percent right. Also, I would feel a lot better knowing the kids will be in our house after the prom.—Concerned Mother

—*ALBUQUERQUE JOURNAL*,
May 15, 1991

Does this scenario sound familiar? It should, because it is played out week after week in living rooms across the country. One side says, "Well, let's be realistic here. They're going to drink anyway. Let's make sure they do it safely." The other side responds, "Alcohol is an illegal drug for any teenager. You are contributing to the delinquency of a minor." What's the answer?

Of all the substances that teenagers ingest illegally, alcohol is by far the most significant. And let's get one thing straight right away: *Alcohol is a drug.* Virtually all high school seniors have tried an alcoholic beverage at least once. In one of the largest national surveys of more than fifteen thousand high school seniors, 60 percent had used alcohol within the previous two weeks. Even more alarming is that one-third of all high school seniors reported having consumed *five or more* drinks in a row during the prior two weeks. A federal government study reported in 1991 that more than a third of the nation's teenagers drink alcohol weekly, and nearly half a million are "binge" drinkers who consume an average of fifteen drinks per week.

Alcohol kills by impairing judgment, whether it involves driving a car or deciding how to cope with one's anger or depression. According to the U.S. Department of Transportation, alcohol was involved in half of the 45,555 traffic deaths in 1989, the last year for which data are available (*Journal of the American Medical Association*, February 6,

1991). Remember that accidents are the leading cause of death among teenagers, accounting for approximately five thousand fatalities per year. In addition, estimates are that alcohol is involved in twenty percent of all suicides and thirty percent of homicides—the next two most important causes of death among teens. We are talking about a drug that is ubiquitous in our society and that is far more likely than cocaine or marijuana to kill you or your teenagers. To phrase it slightly differently, alcohol intoxication is the leading cause of death among teenagers in the United States.

Why do teenagers consume alcohol? One of the primary reasons is that adults do! And for the same reasons: it "relaxes" them, it gives them a "buzz," it helps them to forget about stress, etc. In the 1991 federal government report, 41 percent of the students said they drank when they were upset, 37 percent said they drank to get high, and 30 percent drank when they were bored. Like sex, drinking alcohol is an important privilege and a badge of being an adult. And in our society, adults drink (and make no secret of how much they enjoy drinking). Therefore, role modeling again comes into play, both on a society-wide level and within your family. What kind of attitude do you display toward drugs? I'm not talking about the "nasty" drugs, but about the everyday drugs that we all use: aspirin, caffeine, antibiotics. If you pop a pill every time you've got a headache, that's a behavior that your five-year-old child will quickly learn. If you think it's funny when your spouse gets a little tipsy, your child will think so too.

I'm not saying you have to be an absolute stoic about these things and never touch a pill or a beer in your life. In fact, quite the contrary: One reason why alcohol is not a major problem for many adults is that their parents demystified it for them. They occasionally allowed their children to taste one of their drinks (which, of course, taste awful—alcohol is definitely an acquired taste). When children get to see what the adults are up to, alcohol holds no major attraction for them. It's no longer the forbidden fruit. European parents do the same sort of thing. Children may get a small glass of wine with their meals, just like the grown-ups.

Of course, such parents never gave enough sips for their children to get high, and getting high is another of the most appealing features of drinking for both teenagers and adults. Aside from the "glamour factor" of being able to do something that is both adult and supposedly forbidden to them, teenagers drink for the same reasons as adults: Their friends do it, they want to be sociable and friendly, they like getting high, alcohol can be used to relieve tension or to escape having to deal with problems or conflicts, or simply because drinking makes them feel good. When was the last time you went to a party and your host *didn't* welcome you with "Hi, how are you, what can I get you to drink?" Until very recently, this meant "Which form of alcoholic beverage do you prefer?" Not to mention the fact that newspapers, magazines, and your television screen are all plastered with ads for our favorite intoxicant, made up to look as alluring and benign as possible.

Modern parents should be prepared to be confronted by their children on this issue. I know of many parents whose kids angrily point to their coffee mug in the morning and accuse them of being hooked on drugs. Blind allegiance to the "just say no" mentality makes parents open to such accusations of hypocrisy. Caffeine is indeed a drug, and an addictive one at that! So how should parents respond? I would suggest gently reminding the kids that there are good drugs and bad drugs. Many drugs (such as antibiotics) are life-saving, and others (such as seizure or asthma medications) are necessary to maintain some people's basic level of functioning. And I would cite Aristotle: "All things in moderation." Or pseudo-Shakespeare: One cup of coffee doth not an addict make. Ditto for two aspirins when you've got a bad backache, or two Tylenols for a headache. Young adolescents often think in black-and-white terms, and it's up to you to teach them how to think in grays and in Technicolor. But you can see that your kids are liable to pounce on any drug improprieties of yours, so be very, very careful around them.

By the same token, those of you who have not quit smoking marijuana or using other drugs are fighting a losing and unreasonable battle if you blithely expect your kids to stay away from drugs. Try cleaning up your own act first, before you take it on the road.

Speaking of good drugs and bad drugs, I have met many parents who feel that it's okay for their teenagers— particularly males—to have a keg party at home. "So long as they don't drive" is their usual explanation. Aside from the obvious fact that these people are breaking the law (contributing to the delinquency of a minor), they are also giving their teenagers a very unhealthy message. Yes, I am completely in favor of being realistic; and yes, kids will drink, no matter what we tell them, or how hard we make it for them to get hold of alcoholic beverages. (And we are not making it difficult enough to do that: According to the federal government study, seven million of the seventh-through twelfth-graders who drink buy their own alcoholic beverages, despite the fact that all fifty states have a minimum drinking age of twenty-one.) But the last thing they need from us is a mixed message about this very significant drug.

Getting your kids to "just say no" to drugs illustrates one of the great paradoxes of parenting—one that your parents never had to confront. You are forced to walk a tightrope—too lenient and your kids get permissive-type messages, too conservative and absolute and your kids may well be tipped in the same direction! I am sorry to have to report that there is good research that says teetotaling parents are also at increased risk of producing teenagers with alcohol problems—perhaps because alcohol (like sex) becomes the forbidden fruit. As Twain wrote, "There is a charm about the forbidden that makes it unforgivably desirable." Teenagers are probably more susceptible to this perverse aspect of human psychology than any other age group.

With cigarettes, the advice is easy: Don't smoke—ever! With alcohol, the situation is more complicated. You can't tell your children "Never drink," just as you can't tell them "Never have sex." Alcohol is ubiquitous in American society. It is the most important social lubricant in America today, at parties, at meetings, at business lunches, on dates—the Pennzoil of American society. Once your children reach age twenty-one, they will have free access to alcoholic beverages of all sorts. And, given the statistics, it seems inevitable that they will experiment with alcohol well before that age. So what is the best strategy for you to use?

I think the answer comes with looking at the medical effects of alcohol and the worst-case scenarios. Alcohol is a central nervous system depressant and in low doses is a relaxant, causing impaired judgment and diminished higher cortical functioning. What this means is that it can *lower* your child's inhibitions against having sexual intercourse and certainly impede the ability to drive a car. Teenage girls in particular need to be taught that if they begin drinking socially, they are more likely to wind up in bed with someone they might not ordinarily want to be in bed with, or even become the victim of date rape. They should be taught that the reason they cannot afford to engage in a drinking contest with males is that body weight determines how potent alcohol's effects are: The heavier the person, the less effect a given amount of alcohol will have.

Most parents know that drinking and driving is a problem and that their teenagers may have tried alcohol. Yet the research shows that few parents discuss drinking and driving with their kids, and of those who do, less than 20 percent impose any penalty for drinking and driving. According to the American Academy of Pediatrics, while most parents acknowledge that teenage drinking and driving occurs, only 10 percent believe their own child would do it—it's always "those other kids." Sadly, this is incorrect. In one recent survey of high school seniors, more than 40 percent confessed that in the previous six months they had driven a car after drinking, and nearly 60 percent had ridden in a car with a driver who had been drinking. Parents need to establish an absolute "house rule": "If you ever drink and drive, and if you survive, I will revoke your driver's license. I don't care if you're sixty and I'm eighty-seven. I'm going to come after you and rip it up." Or, as Dr. Cliff Huxtable (Bill Cosby) tells his son Theo about drugs in general: "You know how I feel and how your mother feels about drugs. As long as you are living in this house, *you are not to do any drugs*. When you move into your own house, *you are not to do any drugs*. When I am dead and you're seventy-five, *you are not to do any drugs*."

If you think you can scare your kids away from alcohol by telling them about hepatitis and cirrhosis and alcoholism, save your breath. Only the combination of your own modeling behavior, your firm rules, and some practical information about alcohol can prevent them from becoming another adolescent statistic.

How did Dear Abby reply to Concerned Mother?

Dear Concerned Mother: I vote with your husband. To condone teen-agers drinking beer or any kind of alcoholic beverage in one's home because "they are going to drink anyway" is, in my view, a feeble excuse. Furthermore, providing minors with alcohol is in violation of the law.

If the children were mine, I would insist on hosting the party in my home and providing the snacks, the soft drinks —and the supervision.

Call me old-fashioned if you want, but I am convinced, and many experts agree, that teenagers need and, surprisingly, actually want firmness and clarity about such matters. "Concerned Mother" was being realistic about the risks of drunken driving, but she was also willing to give her son a very inappropriate and unhealthy message: "It's okay to drink when you're sixteen years old." It's not okay. So you see, perhaps parents need to learn to "just say no" before they can expect their kids to!

Marijuana

After alcohol and nicotine, the drug your teenager is most likely to experiment with is marijuana. Here again, some of your own sixties baggage may actually prevent you from being as authoritarian about marijuana as perhaps you should be. But then, American society has had a difficult time trying to cope with its feelings about this drug, and, amazingly, the debate continues even now. This is a classic example of the craziness that can be associated with federal attempts to deal with complicated social issues, as well as the conservative nature of the medical establishment, which is sometimes unwilling to say anything about anything unless there are "smoking gun"–type data available.

Back in 1933, the head of the Federal Bureau of Narcotics stated that marijuana was "physically dangerous,led to insanity, corrupted youth and was as dangerous as heroin." The American Medical Association refused to back him up because, they said, no scientific evidence existed. Three years later, the movie *Reefer Madness* was released —the cautionary and laughable tale of two teenagers who get hooked on the "evil weed." It became a cult classic for many young people in the sixties and seventies who smoked marijuana and gleefully reveled in the fact that they did not become either insane or hooked on heroin. As recently as 1973, the chief drug policy adviser in the White House tried to have marijuana legalized, and even today several experts, including my old friend and high school classmate Mayor Kurt Schmoke of Baltimore, believe that it and other drugs should be legalized.

Much of the problem stems from three facts: The nature of the drug has changed; the much-needed research on marijuana's effects was not done until the 1970s; and adults used scare tactics to keep teenagers away from marijuana. The drug we are talking about in the nineties is not the same drug we smoked in the sixties and early seventies—the potency of the psychoactive ingredient, 9-tetrahydrocannabinol (9-THC), increased at least 250 percent between 1974 and 1989. So what we may have experienced as "a harmless little tickle" is now more of a "mind-bending roar." The most important scientific evidence uncovered about marijuana is that smoking an entire joint is the equivalent of smoking ten cigarettes, from a lung-cancer-causing perspective; marijuana interferes with short-term memory; and, like alcohol, marijuana severely impairs the ability to drive. This is the kind of information that it would benefit children and teenagers to know. Unfortunately, the scientific and educational communities got caught up in the minutiae of scientific research. So in the

1970s we heard all about how marijuana decreases sperm counts and testosterone levels, how pregnant monkeys exposed to marijuana are more likely to abort spontaneously or have offspring with birth defects, and how marijuana turns your brain to mush (later retracted). Such information did not play very well on college campuses across the country, but educators and parents used it in an attempt to scare kids away from the drug. What happened? Instead of scaring kids away, they stimulated kids' curiosity, and marijuana use reached unparalleled levels in 1979 and 1980. By then, nearly two-thirds of high school seniors had tried the drug at least once, and 10 percent admitted to smoking it daily.

Clearly, a lot of people in the late seventies did not believe that marijuana was a dangerous drug. Fortunately, attitudes have changed significantly in the past ten years. The most recent research shows that in 1991 only one-third of high school seniors had ever tried marijuana and 2 percent admitted to using it daily. What has changed in the past ten years? For one thing, we are much smarter about how to educate kids about drugs and prevent them from even experimenting with them (discussed below). For another, kids are finally beginning to understand—as we adults are finally beginning to understand—how dangerous certain drugs like marijuana can be. For example, in the Class of 1991, two-thirds of students now think that trying marijuana even once or twice can be harmful, 80 percent think that smoking it occasionally is bad, and 90 percent think that smoking it regularly is harmful. Back in 1975, fewer than half of high school seniors thought that smoking marijuana occasionally was bad. Those are major changes in attitude over a very short period of time.

Aha, you say—so "just say no" works! Perhaps it does

with drugs like marijuana and cocaine. To the extent that there is much more of an antidrug atmosphere than ever before, there is no doubt that "just say no" has helped. But it certainly hasn't worked with cigarettes and alcohol; and, as we'll see, it still has the potential to backfire badly with other drugs.

What do you tell your kids when they ask about your own drug-taking activities? First, if they don't ask, *don't tell them.* The situation is analogous to telling your spouse that you've had an affair: It may make *you* feel better to make a confession, but it certainly will not make your spouse feel any better, and it's liable to make your relationship a lot more confusing and unstable. As your children's most important role models, you gain nothing by volunteering the information that you were a drug freak in college. Second, if they do ask, there is certainly no need to elaborate on your drug-taking activities in explicit detail. If you tried marijuana, you can simply say that, even if you smoked it every day. Third, "Times *have* changed." Although this phrase is a curse to each new generation, in this particular case it happens to be true. Not only do we now know more about marijuana's effects, but it's a different drug from the one we experimented with. Fourth, be firm and be clear. If you waffle about drugs, your kids will pick up on your ambivalence and not get a clear and consistent message that drugs are bad news. Finally, use the information that is most important to kids and that they most readily accept. Talking about miscarriages in Rhesus monkeys is not going to help you score many points with your kids against marijuana. Likewise, talking about the "amotivational syndrome"— that marijuana basically rots your brain—failed to convince teenagers in the 1970s to stay away from the drug. On the other hand, most teenagers will readily acknowledge that marijuana interferes with short-term memory. So if your child has any academic aspirations whatsoever, she can kiss them good-bye if she starts smoking weed. Similarly, they will acknowledge that marijuana is as dangerous as alcohol if they get behind the wheel of a car after using it, and this impairment can persist for up to twenty-four hours after smoking it. I would also tell kids that smoking *anything* is bad: Lungs weren't made for smoking, and marijuana smoke is a superirritant; smoking a joint is the equivalent of smoking ten cigarettes in terms of carcinogens and tar. Everything else about marijuana I would leave to the scientists to research and debate. Quoting every new medical study to your children does not constitute modern parenting!

Cocaine

On to a really frightening drug—cocaine. With cocaine we have an example of when it is perfectly appropriate to be an absolutist about drugs. We can argue about the merits of letting your nineteen-year-old take a swig of beer from your bottle, or how angry you should be if your teenager tells you that she took one toke on a joint at a party. But there is no arguing about cocaine: Using it even once is the equivalent of putting a bullet in a six-chambered gun, giving it a spin, and firing—Russian roulette. That is because cocaine is a powerful stimulant that in some people (like Len Bias, the Boston Celtics' top draft choice in 1987) can cause an idiosyncratic reaction in the central nervous system that results in seizures and sometimes even death. And there is no way of knowing who is going to have this kind of reaction. Cocaine, along with marijuana and most other street drugs, can also be adulterated with a variety of substances, so that you can never be sure of exactly what you're using. Misjudge the cocaine's purity and you could wind up dead. That is probably what happened to John Belushi, who had himself injected with a mixture of heroin and cocaine (a speedball).

Here is a drug that you probably don't know a lot about; you may not have used it yourself, or have many friends or acquaintances who have used it. Cocaine was around in the sixties, but it was not one of the "drugs of choice" the way marijuana and LSD were. Actually, it still isn't, although you sometimes get that impression from all the media hype about it. Only about 10 percent of the Class of 1990 have ever even tried the drug, and very few can afford to use it daily. It is much more a drug of rich yuppies, athletes, and media stars than of poor high school students.

A three-inch ceramic head of a man with a chewer's bulge, which dates from at least 1500 B.C. and is on display in an Ecuador museum, attests to the fact that natives of the Andean highlands have chewed the leaves of the coca plant for thousands of years. In the Western world the first epidemic use of cocaine came during the 1890s, when it was glamorized by Sherlock Holmes. Sigmund Freud used it. Cocaine was one of the original ingredients of Coca-Cola, but it was removed from the soft drink in the early 1900s. Only during the last decade has cocaine been perceived as a harmful and dangerous drug.

Cocaine is a stimulant that is very similar to amphetamines (speed). Most cocaine users snort cocaine, but it can also be injected intravenously to give a euphoria so intense that it has been compared to an orgasm. This leads to compulsive seeking of the feeling again and again. Laboratory rats allowed unlimited access to it will use it continuously until they die.

Cocaine is available in two forms: a powder, cocaine

hydrochloride; and a base, cocaine freebase, or crack. Crack is powerfully addictive. It is usually smoked, and is cheaper per dose than the powder. This makes it more accessible and desirable to adolescents. Crack can shorten the time from first use to addiction to a matter of weeks.

Cocaine use is self-reinforcing and creates constant drug-seeking behavior once addiction sets in. The need for the drug becomes the sole driving force in the addict's life. Addicted teenagers often run away from home, steal, and become prostitutes. Sporadic use of the drug may produce intense highs and lead to a sense of invulnerability, which predisposes to risk-taking types of behavior. (Needless to say, teenagers don't need this drug when they are already prone to such behaviors without using it.) The intense highs may lead to intense lows once the drug is metabolized, resulting in a need to use other drugs to counterbalance the effects of the cocaine.

The behavior of teenagers who use cocaine can vary in the following ways:

- Wide mood swings and personality changes, associated with early use. A chronically stuffy nose may also be common (but remember that many people, including teenagers, have seasonal allergies, so don't call out the drug-sniffing dogs at the sound of the first sniffle!).
- Regular use, two to three times weekly, will produce intense mood swings, along with falling school grades, changes in the peer group, and interpersonal difficulties at home and school.
- Chronic or daily use will produce a teenager who is withdrawn, depressed, and paranoid and has multiple physical complaints. At any point a full-blown

acute intoxication can occur, with delirium, confusion, paranoia, chest pain, and even seizures and death.

This is not a drug that your teenager is likely to be using *unless* you use it or he is around friends who have access to it. It is a drug that should be avoided at all costs and under all circumstances.

Amphetamines

Cocaine's close cousin, amphetamine, includes such drugs as Benzedrine and Dexedrine, with which many of you may have had some experience, particularly in college. But there is a new stimulant on the block that has caused increased concern in the past several years: crystal methamphetamine, or "ice." Use of ice has been spreading eastward from Hawaii to the West Coast, with usage rates of about 3 percent annually among high school seniors. The euphoria produced by ice is supposedly as intense as that of crack, and it has much more addictive potential than other stimulants. Stimulants, as a group, all cause heightened awareness and alertness, feelings of invulnerability, increased ability to concentrate (at lower doses), and the risk of hypertension, seizures, and even strokes. Like cocaine, amphetamines also have a down side, which may require additional drugs for mood regulation. Amphetamines are bad news, and even casual or experimental use should not be tolerated by parents.

Hallucinogens

Hallucinogens were introduced into American youth culture in the sixties and early seventies by *our* generation. Only we were not seeking to get high—marijuana could do that for us. Rather, we were searching for a better, more peaceful, more humane world, and a higher level of consciousness. You only have to look around to see how successful we were. Meanwhile, the use of LSD spread to younger and younger adolescents, until by the eighties it was more typically used by secondary school students who were merely seeking to get high rather than satisfy any lofty philosophical goals. I am not condoning our generation's use of LSD but rather condoning our *reasons* for wanting to use it. However, now it has become just another drug of abuse.

LSD is one of the most potent substances known, yet, paradoxically, one of the safest in terms of pharmacologic lethality. However, teenagers have been known to be killed while tripping. They fall off rooftops or walk in front of cars. But your strongest argument against LSD (if you used it) is that the drug is now frequently contaminated with a variety of ingredients, some of which can be extremely dangerous—phencyclidine (PCP), for example. Also known as "angel dust" and "hog," PCP produces agitation, hallucinations, muscle rigidity, and seizures. It can be snorted, smoked, ingested, or injected and can act as a stimulant, a depressant, or a hallucinogen, depending on the dose and the means of administration. Overdoses can cause severe aggressive and violent behavior, depression, seizures, coma, and death. This is a drug no person in her right mind would go anywhere near, and if she did, she wouldn't remain in her right mind for very long.

Inhalants

The use of inhalants has always been popular among teenagers because of their easy availability, low cost, legality, and rapid onset of effects. Model airplane glue, paint thinners, nonstick frying sprays—teenagers seeking a high will try inhaling anything they can get their noses to. Approximately 18 percent of high school seniors have tried inhalants at some time, usually as a group activity in which the substance is placed in a plastic bag and the fumes are inhaled. Early changes in consciousness include excitation, euphoria, and exhilaration. However, these may be followed by nausea, vomiting, confusion, disorientation, and eventually loss of coordination, stupor, seizures, and death.

Sedatives and Tranquilizers

Barbiturates, methaqualone (Quaaludes), and benzodiazepines (such as Valium) are categorized as sedatives and tranquilizers. These are central nervous system depressants, which cause a feeling of sleepiness and placidity but in high doses cause respiratory depression. They are both physically and psychologically addictive. Worse yet, in combination with alcohol their effects can be deadly—witness, for example, the famous case of Karen Ann Quinlan, who made the mistake of washing down two Valium tablets with an alcoholic beverage and wound up in an irreversible coma. Teenagers today do not tend to use Quaaludes the way our generation did in the sixties. However, they do use a variety of sedatives and tranquilizers in conjunction with stimulants, to bring them down from their highs.

Narcotics

With the exception of certain high-risk groups in major urban centers, teenagers do not commonly use or even experiment with narcotics such as heroin. Although addiction is not automatic, recurrent use ensures an increased tolerance and a craving for more drug. The intravenous use of heroin (or any drug) not only exposes the user to the risk of HIV, it may result in other serious and life-threatening illnesses, such as hepatitis or infection of the heart valves. And, again, because of the variability in both the dose and the composition of these drugs, harmful reactions and overdoses are extremely common and occur unpredictably. As with cocaine, teenagers who are heavily involved with narcotics frequently have to resort to stealing, dealing, or prostitution to support their habit.

"HOW DO I KNOW IF MY SON OR DAUGHTER IS DOING DRUGS?"

❏

CLARK: *As described by his parents, Clark is a fourteen-year-old who has always been a "so-so" student. He thinks that school is "boring" and would prefer to socialize with his friends or play baseball. He is a superb pitcher and wants to play in the major leagues after high school. His parents very much want him to go to college. His mother graduated from college and has a master's degree in teaching. His father is a pathologist. They have had Clark tested, and he has an average IQ. Clark's parents have come to see me, without bringing him, to discuss the possibility of having a drug screen done. They are worried that he is "hanging out with the wrong crowd." Also, they heard an expert on the radio say that parents need to worry if their kids are doing poorly in school.*

In talking with Clark's parents, I find that they are describing a young teenager who has been progressing along his own path at a slow but constant rate. His grades have always been C's, and he is well behaved in school

*and does all of his homework. His closest friends seem
trustworthy to Clark's parents. Clark does not smoke, nor
do his parents. They occasionally drink wine with meals,
but Clark shows little interest in it. He is reliable in doing
his chores, shows no oppositional behavior with them or
his teachers, and simply appears to be a teenager who is
not gifted intellectually. I explain to them that not only do
I not favor doing drug testing on teenagers, I do not think
that their son is at especially high risk. However, I will be
happy to talk with Clark to do an evaluation.*

❏

"How do I know if my son or daughter is doing drugs?"
This is a surprisingly common question for parents of our
generation. Theoretically, this should not be difficult,
since we used drugs ourselves and therefore should be
able to spot many of the telltale signs: evasiveness,
changes in moods or habits or friends, lying, stealing
money, breaking curfew, etc. But the statistics are alarming, and all parents—even sophisticated ones—must constantly be on guard. So let me tell you some of the tricks
of the trade.

The first trick, as we'll discuss in chapter 7, is to use
your pediatrician or family physician as an ally: If he is
sensitive to the principles of adolescent medicine, then he
can perform a drug screen for you—*not* a urine test, mind
you; rather, he will simply ask your teenager what drugs,
if any, she is using. Although he will have to keep this
information confidential, at least you will be reassured
that an intelligent and caring adult knows about your
teenager's drug involvement and will be trying to make
an effective intervention. Of course, you can try asking
your teenager yourself. As with asking about sex, some

teenagers will respond to a direct approach; others will prefer a more indirect approach. With kids in their early to mid-adolescence, asking about their peer group will be tantamount to asking about their own activity. With older teenagers this will not always be true, since they have the ability to tolerate certain behaviors among their friends that they themselves would not necessarily feel comfortable doing. Few teenagers will be threatened by a question such as "Are drugs a problem at your school?" In fact, you'll probably get more accurate answers to this question from your kids than from school officials, who will categorically deny that *their* school has a problem, although they will readily acknowledge that drugs are a problem in *other* schools (school administrators' version of the personal fable).

The second trick is that different drugs have different manifestations. Cigarettes are easy: You can smell it on their breath and on their clothes. And if your teenager doesn't smoke by age fifteen or sixteen, it is unlikely that he ever will. But, as I have said before, cigarettes are probably the single most important gateway drug, and I would not minimize the impact they can have on your adolescent's health in general and, specifically, on the possible progression to other drugs. Smoking is also a filthy, expensive, unhealthy habit. I would be just as upset if my children started smoking as if I found out they were popping Quaaludes.

Alcohol use is also relatively easy to spot, but, unfortunately, many parents tend to condone its use, as illustrated in the "Dear Abby" letter. Kids may come home drunk or high, especially after weekend parties. How you respond to finding your inebriated teenager on your doorstep at one o'clock on Saturday morning may determine her future drug-taking course. If you laugh it off as "just one of those adolescent things," her behavior is unlikely to change. On the other hand, if you take such behavior seriously and refuse to condone it, she is more likely to perceive that her drinking will have very real negative consequences for her.

Let's say your normally reliable and upstanding sixteen-year-old son comes home drunk after a party. You hear him retching on your doorstep. He has alcohol on his breath and is barely coherent. You are angry that he has been experimenting with alcohol, even angrier that he has managed to get himself drunk, and acutely disappointed in him for letting you down. How should you handle this situation? The possibilities include (A) Do nothing. (B) Get some hot coffee into him to help sober him up. (C) Ground him for the rest of his life. (D) Yell at him for being irresponsible. (E) Make him sleep outside until he sobers up.

You may be surprised to learn that the best answer is (A) Do nothing—at least not until the next morning! As we'll talk about later, punishing in anger is counterproductive to what you are actually trying to accomplish, which is to see that the behavior does not occur again—*not* to inflict pain and suffering. The next day, talk with your son and investigate the circumstances of the drinking. The most crucial question is, was he driving? If so, the consequences should be particularly severe (such as losing his driving privileges for an extended period of time). If he wasn't driving, who drove him home? Was that person drunk as well? Again, if the answer is yes, the punishment should be severe. Next, why didn't your son call you to come pick him up? I advise most parents to negotiate a "no penalty" contract with their teenagers, an agreement that they will come pick the kids up wherever and whenever necessary, no questions asked, if they are intoxicated. Call it "no-fault insurance":

CONTRACT FOR LIFE

A Contract for Life Between Parent and Teenager

Under this contract, we understand S.A.D.D. encourages all youth to adopt a *no use* policy and obey the laws of their state with regard to alcohol and illicit drugs.

Teenager   I agree to call you for advice and/or transportation at any hour from any place if I am ever faced with a situation where a driver has been drinking or using illicit drugs. I have discussed with you and fully understand your attitude toward any involvement with underage drinking or the use of illegal drugs.

_____
Signature

Parent   I agree to come and get you at any hour, any place, no questions asked and no argument at that time, or I will pay for a taxi to bring you home safely. I expect we would discuss this at a later time.

I agree to seek safe, sober transportation home if I am ever in a situation where I have had too much to drink or a friend who is driving me has had too much to drink.

_____
Signature

_____
Date

Distributed by S.A.D.D., "Students Against Driving Drunk"

In the above example, I would also want to know exactly what his experience with alcohol has been up to now: Was this his first episode of drinking, or has he been experimenting for some time? If the answer is the latter, I would phone my pediatrician or family physician immediately to make an appointment for an evaluation. Finally, how was the alcohol obtained: someone's phony ID? parents? older friends? There may be mitigating circumstances involved, and you'd be surprised how many otherwise intelligent parents are willing to serve as bartenders for their underage children.

The most important principles here are to avoid overreacting and to resist the temptation to punish in anger. Given the statistics on adolescent drug use, the fact that your son or daughter tries alcohol should not surprise you —more than 90 percent of teenagers do before they graduate from high school. But being able to anticipate such behavior does not necessarily mean that you have to condone it. Teaching children appropriate limits has always been one of the crucial jobs of parenting.

It is important for parents to know, and to teach their children, that once alcohol is ingested, there is no way to increase its rate of metabolism. Strong black coffee and cold showers to try to sober someone up are absolutely useless. This is one of those myths that have been perpetuated in the movies and on TV shows for decades. You drink it and you're stuck with it until your liver can detoxify it. This is the reason that every year some foolish fraternity pledge dies from acute alcohol poisoning—he downs half a quart of vodka, feels fine, and finishes off the bottle. Two hours later, he's dead.

Many of us already know how to spot marijuana use, since we tried to cover up the clues when we were teenagers, or remember our friends getting stoned: red eyes, dilated pupils, a craving for munchies, the acrid smell, the smoking accessories, etc. What most parents don't realize is that any heavy involvement with marijuana, cocaine, uppers, downers, or narcotics can be suspected early—if there is a deterioration in school performance. The recurrent use of marijuana or any of the harder drugs will impair teenagers' short-term memory and their ability to concentrate, making it virtually impossible to perform effectively in school. School performance can serve as a very sensitive index to your teenager's well-being in general. After all, she has had eight or ten years of schooling already and has established a track record. A student who typically gets all B's and suddenly is getting C's and D's is sending out a unique kind of distress signal. Of course, at this point other clues will probably be present as well: new friends, furtive use of the phone, coming and going at unusual hours, disappearance of household money. Heavy involvement in drugs means that drug-seeking behavior beings to dominate all free time. But before teenagers reach this stage, remember that their schoolwork is probably a more sensitive index of drug abuse than even a urine drug screen. Why? Because, contrary to popular belief, doctors aren't omniscient and can't detect every malady, even using modern, sophisticated tests. You can't just take a sample of urine, run it through a machine, and come up with the magic answer. Some drugs don't stay in the system very long, some require very expensive equipment and tests have to be requested specifically for that substance, and some drugs can be detected only in minute amounts that are below the screening capabilities of most machines. You have to program the machine for whatever substances you are looking for. And if you try to screen for everything, the cost is astronomical. Not to mention the fact that if you secretly try to test your teenager against his will, you will have lost whatever few remaining bonds of trust existed.

This brings us to a very sensitive area of discussion, a real gray area for parents and professionals alike: When is it appropriate to search a teenager's room for evidence of drug use? I hope that I have made a good case for parents being astute diagnosticians early in the course of drug involvement, and for using the pediatrician or family physician—on a yearly basis—to help assess the teenager's well-being and risk factors. So my answer to this question is that rarely should it even be necessary to undertake a search mission in your teenager's room. If you are considering such tactics, understand that you would completely devastate your relationship with your teenager and completely abrogate her sense of trust in you. You must also be ready to have your teenager hospitalized in an inpatient adolescent drug treatment facility, should your worst fears be confirmed. Having said this, there is an important principle in medicine: "Never say never." So I can't tell you that I would *never* advocate searching a teenager's room. But I would hope that any drug involvement could be detected much earlier and more efficiently without Operation Bedroom Storm.

DRUG-ABUSE PREVENTION

Besides your pediatrician or family physician, you have other allies in the fight against drugs, among them your fellow parents and your community, especially schools. Prevention efforts need to begin at home, but they certainly shouldn't end there. As with sex education, there is a real need for school- and community-wide involvement, too. But it's more complicated than a simple "just say no" campaign. Let's look at some of the intricacies of drug-abuse prevention, including some of the reasons why teenagers become involved with drugs in the first place, and then how you might think about getting involved in some prevention efforts of your own.

Parents

We've already talked about role modeling and parental attitudes. Do you allow smoking in your house? If so, be prepared for a battle from your smoking teenagers, because they will accuse you of hypocrisy if you allow your friends to smoke in the house but refuse to allow *them* to smoke. How do you react to a falling-down drunk portrayed on television? Do you think it's funny when people talk about getting "wasted" or "bombed," or the need to "party hearty"? If you condone the attitudes portrayed in beer and wine advertising—alcohol makes everything more fun—then your kids will certainly feel the same way. What kind of parties do you have in your house? Younger children are invariably fascinated by their parents' parties and like to watch how adults entertain themselves and one another. Do you greet your guests with a glass in your hand?

The parent-adolescent relationship is also a crucial determinant of whether or not the teenager will experiment with drugs. A happy, secure, well-balanced teenager who feels close to his parents is at low risk for heavy involvement in drugs. Similarly, a teenager who has already gotten her risk-taking needs met in socially acceptable ways (skiing, scuba diving, Outward Bound activities) will not feel the "need for speed" (to quote Tom Cruise's character in *Top Gun*). Teenagers who are heavily involved in athletic or religious activities are also at low risk, with the exception of certain sports associated with the use of anabolic steroids.

The prevention of alcohol use, in particular, is one of the most important successes that parents can have, but only if they band together. As I have said many times, there are far too many parents willing to supply their kids with beer for parties. But if you establish contacts with all of the parents of your teenager's friends, and you all agree that alcohol at parties is off-limits and that parties need some sort of adult supervision at all times, then you have effectively created a unique kind of "peer pressure" of your own. You have completely annihilated one of your kid's favorite arguments: "Well, Johnny's parents let *him* do it." It is crucial to remove this kind of temptation—the empty house, the unlocked liquor cabinet, etc.—from teenagers. Your supply of beer and liquor at home must be kept *locked up*, not because you don't trust your teenager, but because alcohol is a serious drug and he doesn't need the temptation of an unlocked liquor cabinet.

Safe Rides

A number of communities have established Safe Ride programs, in which teenagers who have been drinking late at night can phone a special number for a free ride home. Often these programs are sponsored by such organizations as Mothers Against Drunk Driving (MADD) and teen groups like Students Against Driving Drunk (SADD). They are the community equivalent of the parent-teenager contract we talked about previously and accomplish the same purpose: to insulate teenagers against the most hazardous aspect of drinking—driving afterward. Some adults may complain that this represents a double standard, much the same as allowing free access to birth control for teenagers; but, again, it is difficult to conceive of how offering a free ride home is going to encourage anyone to drink. Teenagers are not particularly future-oriented and tend not to worry about the consequences of their current actions. As with sex, the decision about whether to drink is rooted firmly in the family, peers, and individual psychology. Safe Ride programs simply ensure that kids get home safely without having to get behind the wheel of a car, endangering themselves, their passengers, and innocent sober people. Given the choice between having a drunk teenager delivered safely home and a dead teenager delivered to the morgue—similar to the choice between having a teenager use contraception or becoming a grandparent—no parent is going to choose the former option.

Why "Just Say No" Just Won't Work

Concerned parents also need to become involved in community and school prevention programs, particularly because some are ineffective and others may actually backfire. This is where "just say no" comes into play. In its simplest and therefore most commonly used form, "just say no" is an insult to every teenager in America. Imagine if adults had tried to perpetrate something like that on our generation—we would have laughed our heads off. Don't get me wrong: We all agree that teenagers *should* say no to drugs. Unfortunately, "just say no" is an overly simplistic attempt to solve a very complex problem. As *part* of a much more intensive and thoughtful effort, it may have some legitimacy. There is no question that the change in society's attitude reflected in the "just say no" philosophy has helped to make a dent in the adolescent drug problem during the past decade. The use of drugs such as marijuana and LSD has declined dramatically. But we will need more than just a slogan to be truly effective.

Where did "just say no" come from in the first place? Americans are famous for trying to find quick and easy solutions to complex problems. But how can teaching a slogan to children make any difference in their decision whether to use drugs, when that decision is based upon a very complex interaction between their own self-image and personality, their relationships with their parents and peers, the media, and society in general? If parents are content to let a slogan do all the work for them, they will quickly find that the "just say no" approach has no basis in scientific fact; it contains several major elements of hypocrisy; it ignores the basic principles of adolescent psychology; it may be crowding out much better—but more costly and labor-intensive—drug-use-prevention programs; and it ignores the two most important drugs that adolescents use—alcohol and cigarettes.

No Scientific Basis. To date, there has been no scientific study documenting the effectiveness of the "just say no" campaign. On the other hand, several informal surveys have shown that teenagers, in particular, may resent such an approach. Yet millions of dollars are being poured into "just say no" campaigns. If the National Institutes of Health gave millions of dollars to some program that had never been field-tested, Congress and the American public would be in an uproar.

The "just say no" philosophy hovers dangerously close to the scare tactics that were tried on us when we were teenagers. In our day, parents and teachers used to think that if they could only succeed in educating us about the dangers of drugs, we would stay away from using them. (There are some interesting parallels here with sex education.) But that education often consisted of the "God will strike you dead if you try it" approach. In the early 1970s a child psychiatrist in Seattle decided to test this sort of approach. He studied kids at two different high schools, one with a scare program and the other with no program at all. He then examined drug use by teenagers in both schools, before and after the scare program was established—and found that the high school students exposed to the scare program actually used more drugs, not less!

This "boomerang" effect surprised researchers, but it shouldn't have. It simply showed the wonderful contrariness of normal adolescents! Other factors may have been important as well: The scare program may have made it seem that all teenagers were using drugs, so the kids who weren't began to feel some imaginary peer pressure. It may have increased their curiosity about certain drugs. Whatever caused the boomerang effect, we now know that fear is a powerful emotion that is completely inappropriate in trying to motivate teenagers to avoid drugs.

Hypocrisy. Because the "just say no" campaign has targeted primarily marijuana and the harder drugs and completely ignored cigarettes and alcohol, it has been criticized as hypocritical. After all, if you imply that kids should never drink alcohol, how strong an argument can you make for adults drinking it as frequently as they do? None of those very clever Partnership for a Drug Free America ads ("This is your brain. This is your brain on drugs. Any questions?") attacks alcohol or cigarettes. Corporate America clearly has a major financial stake in having teenagers "just say yes" to cigarettes and beer and wine when they become adults. But, of course, adults first learned to smoke and drink as teenagers. And, as we'll see in the next chapter, many of the advertisements for cigarettes and alcohol are actually directed at young people, despite manufacturers' protestations that they would never stoop so low. Teens may also find it ironic to see their favorite rock star or sports star doing a public service announcement for "just say no" one week and then hear about a celebrity in a related field being arrested for drunken driving or cocaine possession a week later. Consider also the fact that in 1987 the U.S. Government invested about $300 million a year in drug-use-prevention campaigns and strategies, yet the next year it paid $500 million to tobacco farmers. Beer and wine manufacturers spend $900 million a year on advertising. Cigarette manufacturers spend over $6 billion a year on cigarette advertising (just not on television ads). This is all beginning to look like a scene out of *Alice in Wonderland:* The faster we run, the behinder we get. We are creating a massive problem and trying to clean it up at the same time.

Normal Psychology. It doesn't take a specialist in adolescent medicine to tell you the obvious: Not only do teenagers resent being told what to do, they may react by doing precisely the opposite. Parents have often compared their kids' adolescence with the "terrible twos." What "just say no" says to the average teenager is "You have no identity of your own. You are programmable. We know what is best for you. We will control the horizontal; we will control the vertical. [Remember *Outer Limits*?] You will do exactly as we tell you to do." The slogan is just that—a slogan. It does not teach teenagers *why* they should say no or give them the skills to know *how* they should say no. In short, it treats them like children, which is one of the biggest mistakes you can make in trying to deal effectively with teenagers.

Successful Prevention Programs. Increasing numbers of drug prevention programs *have* undergone close scientific scrutiny and *have* been shown to be effective. Many of these programs target cigarettes and alcohol as well as marijuana and other drugs. They use a far more sophisticated, social-psychological approach to drug-use-prevention, based on social learning theory and the notion of "psychological inoculation." Social learning theory states that new behaviors originate, on a trial basis, from chance exposures to powerful role models. For example, young smokers may be trying to emulate their parents, their peers, or attractive role models they see in the media. The concept of psychological inoculation suggests that if a person encounters "germs" (social pressures to adopt an unhealthy behavior), you can prevent "infection" by giving that person a weak vaccinating dose to produce "antibodies" (skills for resisting pressure). The result is a blend of drug education, assertiveness training, and media criticism that can increase resistance to drugs. One such pilot program, in San Jose, California, demonstrated more than a 50 percent reduction in new cigarette smokers, drinkers, and pot smokers during a two-year followup period. In suburban New York, one researcher used a "life skills" approach for eighth- to tenth-graders that included cognitive teaching, decision-making skills, training in coping with stress and anxiety, social skills development, and self-improvement projects. After one year, cigarette smoking by new smokers had been reduced by 50 percent. After a "booster" session was added, an 87 percent reduction was achieved at the end of two years. A related study showed a reduction in marijuana use of 71 percent.

Clearly, we've come a long way. But if these programs have been shown to be so successful, why haven't they been implemented in every school district across the country? For one thing, not everybody knows about these sorts of programs, and there is always the uniquely human failing of wanting to reinvent the wheel. Second, school administrators are notoriously slow to implement any new ideas, especially if money is required. Such programs *are* costly and labor-intensive, and must be accompanied by a research type of evaluation design to document that they are doing what they are intended to do. "Just say no," on the other hand, requires some buttons and bumper stickers and a few public service announcements for the local radio and TV stations. In other words, we have a Gresham's law of drug-use-prevention programs—the bad programs could be driving out the good ones. In addition, children and teenagers are not all alike, nor are they susceptible to the same tactics. It is entirely possible that "just say no" clubs could be effective with third-graders. It is also possible that such an approach would boomerang with eleventh-graders. Programs must be designed that are age-specific. "Just say no," on the other hand, is a "one size fits all" concept.

Alcohol and Cigarettes. Although alcohol and cigarettes are the biggest threat to your child's health, "just say no" never deals with either. Between sixty and one hundred million Americans currently use cigarettes and alcohol, compared with less than 5 percent as many who use cocaine or heroin, the two most dangerous illicit drugs. Yet on television you get the impression that cocaine is the number one killer in America today. The number of people dying from cocaine use is probably in the hundreds, and no one dies from using marijuana. If we want to get our kids to "just say no," then at least let's point them in the right direction!

Getting kids to stay away from drugs requires a major effort, and it must begin at home, at an early age. But at any age, prevention is far easier than treatment. Getting kids off drugs is a separate issue, one that we will discuss in chapter 7. Now more than ever your children need clear messages from you about drug use and sex—activities that we once thought were merely amusing, but now can be life-threatening.

Chapter 5

Television: The New Substitute Parent

❑

Television will be of no importance in your lifetime or mine.

—BERTRAND RUSSELL

If the home is to become a non-stop movie house, God help the home.

—ORSON WELLES

Chewing gum for the eyes.

—FRANK LLOYD WRIGHT

Sincerity is the thing that comes through on television.

—RICHARD NIXON

We are the first media generation. Do these names sound at all familiar: Rocky and Bullwinkle, Lucy Ricardo, Dr. Richard Kimble, Eliot Ness, Howdy Doody, Buffalo Bob, Beaver Cleaver, Miss Nancy, Rod Serling, Napoleon Solo? Does the name Ruby Begonia ring a bell? We were the first kids to grow up with television. Consequently, we should be the first generation to really appreciate how television has profoundly changed the way children grow up and how crucial the media in general have become in our lives. Yet it is precisely because we grew up with television that many of us fail to recognize how important it is in our children's lives. We are now busy adults, many of us with full-time careers, and we may not watch very much TV anymore. We may assume that what's on today doesn't differ very much from what we watched as kids. But that would be a rather foolish assumption indeed. Moreover, because we are so busy, and because many of our families are in such a state of flux from divorce and remarriage, television has now become the newest member of the family—the substitute parent that teaches our kids all the wrong things about sex and alcohol and violence and the adult world. No parents in their right minds would invite a stranger into the house to teach their kids about such sensitive subjects for three to five hours a day, yet television is doing precisely that.

We grew up during the golden age of television. Shows like *Leave It to Beaver*, *The Donna Reed Show*, *I Love Lucy*, *The Mickey Mouse Club*, and *Father Knows Best* glorified the sanctity of the family and taught wholesome, family values. If your parents parked you in front of the TV set for an hour or two, they knew you were safe and in good hands. Unfortunately, that is no longer the case. The United States has the worst programming for children in the world—the most violent, the most sexually irresponsible, the most commercially exploitive. Worse, there is a direct relationship between the media and such major teenage problems as premature sexual intercourse, alcohol use, and suicide. So if you want your teenagers to grow up happy and healthy, it is essential that you, as a modern parent, understand what role television and other media play in their lives and how you can at least minimize the negative impact that they can have.

At this juncture, you are probably thinking that I am some sort of Bible-thumping antitelevision evangelist. It might surprise you to learn that I love television and movies, when they're good. I grew up with a TV set in my bedroom—one of those old-time models with a thirteen-inch screen set into a box that was three times the size—and watched a lot of television as a kid; some of my family and friends work in various media; I am a published novelist; and my research interest is the effects of the media on children and adolescents and how the media can be used as a *positive* health influence. In other words, I feel strongly that television not only is part of the problem but also can be part of the solution. With a few exceptions, the media are neither intrinsically good or bad—they are what we make them. Unfortunately, in 1993, in the United States, the media are overwhelmingly more bad than good.

WHY TELEVISION IS SO IMPORTANT

Of all the media, television ranks as the most significant. Consider these statistics: By the time today's children reach age seventy, they will have spent *seven years* watching television. Children and teenagers spend more time watching television (fifteen to eighteen thousand hours) than they do in formal classroom instruction (twelve thousand hours). Kids spend more time watching television than in any other activity except sleeping! According to the Nielsen ratings, American children average twenty-two to twenty-six hours a week watching television, or an average of three to four hours a day. (Although this seems phenomenally high, children are not the worst offenders: Women over the age of fifty-five watch forty-four hours a week, and men over the age of fifty-five average thirty-seven hours a week.) In an average year, American children view:

- Nearly 14,000 sexual references, innuendoes, and jokes, with fewer than 175 of them related to responsible sexuality
- More than 1,000 rapes, homicides, and assaults
- Nearly 2,000 beer and wine commercials
- Approximately 20,000 other commercials

Television has completely broken through the boundaries of the American family. Before our generation, if your parents told you something, you had no way of corroborating it, other than by talking with your friends. But beginning in the 1950s, kids who watched television suddenly were exposed to the "real world" at a very early age, and TV shows gave them secret glimpses of how adults "really" think and behave. This is why television is one of the most powerful educators of children today, and it's a very opportunistic medium. If you don't teach your kids what they want to know, television will be happy to step in and fill the void. The problem is that TV may be teaching your kids what *you* don't want them to know about.

People tend to grossly underestimate the influence of the media in their lives. This may occur for a number of reasons. No intelligent person likes to admit for a moment to actually watching television, much less being influenced by it. Television is also so ubiquitous that we sometimes forget it's even there, or how important it is. More American households have TV sets than indoor plumbing, for example. In one study, researchers found that 60 percent of families had changed their sleeping patterns because of television, and 55 percent had altered mealtimes. I have treated teenagers who live in families with a TV set in each bedroom; at mealtimes, family members dish up the food in the kitchen and then adjourn to their own rooms to watch their favorite shows. In New York City, when the Super Bowl was first televised the water pressure in the sewer system dropped to dangerously low levels because everyone was going to the bathroom during the commercials! We sometimes forget how TV and movie personalities have crept into our everyday lives. For example, you might be surprised to learn that in the first 150 pages of this book there are nearly a hundred media references. It has become a kind of shorthand way of communicating with each other. Think about such famous expressions (in chronological order) as "How sweet it is" (Jackie Gleason); "The devil made me do it" (Flip Wilson); "Sock it to me" and "Very interesting" (*Laugh-In*); "Sit on it" (the Fonz on *Happy Days*); "Never mind" (Roseanne Roseannadanna of *Saturday Night Live*). Soitenly, as Curley of the Three Stooges would say. Schoolchildren, too, use media characters to communicate with each other and to organize their play activities. For this reason—as well as the fact that TV *can* be educational—it is unwise for parents simply to toss the TV set out the window. My wife grew up without a TV set in the house, and I can tell you that she's the last person in the world you'd want to have as a Trivial Pursuit partner.

Many adults don't like to think about the media's impact, because once they acknowledge it the implications are positively Orwellian. George Orwell always thought that in 1984 Big Brother would be watching us, but in fact we were watching Big Brother—the TV set. Too many parents still use the television set as an electronic baby sitter, and they would like to believe that their children are not being harmed by it.

A number of events in our lifetime attest to the power of the media. Who can forget the Kennedy-Nixon debates, or Kennedy's assassination, or the sight of Jack Ruby killing Lee Harvey Oswald on live TV? In 1980 and again in 1984, Americans chose a former movie star (and a master manipulator of the media) as their President. More recently, Michael Dukakis confessed that he made a "major mistake" in the 1988 presidential race by underestimating the power of television and the importance of the "sound bite." In the 1968 campaign, sound bites lasted an average of 42 seconds; by 1988 that figure had dropped to 9.8 seconds. Dukakis claimed that "if you couldn't say it in less than 10 seconds, it wasn't heard because it wasn't aired" (*New York Times*, April 22, 1990). Have we now reached a point in American politics at which the person who manipulates the media the best wins? In case you think this discussion of politics applies only to adults, consider a study of suburban Maryland children that found they could identify more alcoholic beverages by brand name than American Presidents.

Parents may also underestimate TV's power over children because they mistakenly think that children watch TV the way adults do. They think that children understand that TV is fantasy and entertainment, not "real life." Unfortunately, this is precisely the opposite of what actually occurs: To children, especially two- to eight-year-olds, television *is* real. Children lack adults' reasoning abilities and their experience in the real world. Consequently, they view the television world as being realistic, and it shapes their behaviors accordingly. Television gives them all sorts of useful information about how adults behave, ranging from what makes adults successful (white-collar jobs and money, generally) to how adults relax (with a beer and a burp) and how adults have sex (frequently, with people they scarcely know and without using birth control).

HOW TV INFLUENCES BEHAVIOR

"You people sit there, night after night. You're beginning to believe this illusion we're spinning here. You're beginning to think the tube is reality and your own lives are unreal. This is mass madness!"

—Anchorman HOWARD BEALE,
in Paddy Chayevsky's *Network*

Contrary to popular belief, people rarely imitate directly and immediately what they see in the media. When they do, it makes headlines. For instance, when the award-winning movie *The Deer Hunter* was released, several teenagers across the country killed themselves after playing Russian roulette (imitating a powerful scene from the movie, which starred Robert De Niro). More recently, a young Iowa girl was killed after running in front of a train (mimicking a scene from the popular Stephen King movie *Stand by Me*, which her friends said she was obsessed with). These kinds of examples occur rarely—although the fact that they occur at all should tell you something. Instead, television has a much more subtle and insidious effect, shaping kids' attitudes and perceptions. TV offers kids "scripts" about gender roles, conflict resolution, and patterns of courtship and sexual gratification that they may not be able to observe anywhere else. For example, if you are a mother, much of your image of what constitutes an ideal mother may have been shaped not only by your own mother but also by television's ideal mothers: Betty Anderson, June Cleaver, Clair Huxtable, even Edith Bunker. And even if your own image hasn't been affected, much of your children's image of what you *should* be like may be shaped by these fictional characters. This kind of influence is particularly powerful if people watch a lot of TV. It is known as the "cultivation effect"—the belief that the TV world is real and people in everyday life should behave accordingly.

Remember that children learn from imitating attractive adult role models, and there are no adult role models more attractive than what can be viewed on the screen in your living room. So if you are not as available to your kids as perhaps you should be or would like to be, please be advised that there are plenty of adult parent-type role models ready to do your job for you. Of course, television provides ample opportunities for both good and bad behaviors to be learned through modeling—for example, nonviolent resolution of conflicts, rather than the acceptability of violence if you're the "good guy." Unfortunately, at present American television is rife with examples of unhealthy behaviors for children and adolescents and contains precious few examples of prosocial modeling.

When adult society refuses to permit widespread dissemination of information (such as sex education in school), the media also may serve as an important *source of information*, albeit a frequently inaccurate one. Because of the sheer number of hours that kids spend in front of the television set, TV also exerts a *displacement effect*. In other words, other, less passive activities like reading and sports are shortchanged. Even if TV were harmless, the time spent watching it would be highly significant.

Ten Specific Areas of Influence

1. Aggressive Behavior

> *"If parents could buy packaged psychological influences to administer in regular doses to their children, I doubt that many would deliberately select Western gun slingers, hopped-up psychopaths, deranged sadists, slap-stick buf-*

foons and the like, unless they entertained rather peculiar ambitions for their growing offspring. Yet such examples of behavior are delivered in quantity, with no direct charge, to millions of households daily. Harried parents can easily turn off demanding children by turning on a television set; as a result, today's youth is being raised on a heavy dosage of televised aggression and violence."

—TV researcher ALBERT BANDURA
(*Look* magazine, 1963)

More than a thousand studies and reviews attest to the fact that exposure to heavy doses of TV violence increases the likelihood of aggressive behavior, particularly among males. Two official U.S. Government reports have confirmed this—the Surgeon General's Report in 1972 and the report of the National Institutes of Mental Health in 1982. Ask any kindergarten or elementary school teacher —she can practically recite the entries in *TV Guide* for you, based on the behavior she observes the next morning on the playground. The connection between violence on TV and aggressive behavior in children is so well confirmed that communications researchers aren't even interested in studying it anymore. Yet the networks continue to claim that nothing has been proven yet! They simply want to make a lot of money by showing action shows, without taking the responsibility for the repercussions of all the violence portrayed. And the quantity of violence on American prime-time TV shows has not changed appreciably in the past ten years, despite all that we now know about its harmful effects.

Are all kids vulnerable to violence on TV? Yes. Are all kids equally affected by it? No. Much depends on what kind of job you are doing raising your kids, whether you watch and discuss TV programs with them, and whether they are male or female (boys are far more susceptible than girls to the effects of TV violence). Also, if parents are loving and discourage aggressive behavior, their kids are less likely to be aggressive or to be influenced by violent programming.

What, precisely, is bad about TV violence? Aside from the fact that children are liable to imitate it, TV violence gives kids misleading information about human behavior. For example, according to TV all crises can be resolved within twenty-three or forty-six minutes (the actual amount of programming in a half-hour or hour show, respectively). Likewise, violence is an acceptable solution to very complex problems, especially if you're the good guy wearing the white hat.

Television is such a ubiquitous influence that we are not even aware that our attitudes have been changed by it. As writer Michael Arlen commented in *Living Room War* (Viking Press, 1969), his book about television coverage of the Vietnam War:

> I can't say I completely agree with people who think that when battle scenes are brought into the living room the hazards of war are necessarily made "real" to the civilian audience. It seems to me that by the same process they are also made less "real"—diminished, in part, by the physical size of the television screen, which, for all the industry's advances, still shows one picture of men three inches tall shooting at other men three inches tall, and trivialized, or at least tamed, by the enveloping cozy alarums of the household.

I talk with a lot of parents who understand how violent TV is and, like schoolteachers, can tell when their kids have been watching violent cartoons or prime-time action shows. But others sometimes ask, "Well, Dr. Strasburger, I grew up watching Hopalong Cassidy and Roy Rogers and Road Runner cartoons, and I am not a particularly violent or aggressive person. How do your theories apply to me?" My response is: "Either you are one of those people who were less susceptible to TV violence, because of the way your parents raised you, or you are simply unaware of how violent programming has actually shaped some of your fundamental attitudes and beliefs." As researcher L. Rowell Huesmann concluded (in the *Journal of Social Issues*, Vol. 42, 1986):

> Aggressive habits seemed to be learned early in life, and, once established, are resistant to change and predictive of serious adult antisocial behavior. If a child's observations of media violence promotes the learning of aggressive habits, it can have *lifelong* consequences. [Emphasis added.]

2. Commercialization and Consumerism

> *"It shall be a crime punishable by death to sell anything to a child without power of attorney."*
>
> —Code of HAMMURABI,
> c. 2250 B.C.

American television is the most commercially exploitive of children of any broadcasting medium in the Western world. Toy manufacturers make an estimated $40 million a year pitching their products to children who are psychologically defenseless. Young children are incapable of understanding the true intent of commercials and believe that their claims are real. To date, more than seventy programs have been developed in which the product came first and the program was an afterthought, designed to sell more of the product. These "program-length commercials" often glamorize war toys (*He-Man and Masters of the Universe, Rambo, G.I. Joe*). More than four thousand years after the Code of Hammurabi, selling products to children has become "business as usual." At the same time, the United States is the only Western nation that does not produce at least one hour a day of educational programming for children on its national commercial networks. It is odd that we often complain about how our children are becoming little consumers, yet take no action to stop it from happening. And we don't use television to its fullest potential as an educational tool. Rather, television programming exists solely to deliver an audience to advertisers.

Commercialism is now creeping into the classroom as well. Channel One, a business venture of Whittle Communications, offers school systems fifty thousand dollars' worth of free video equipment if they will broadcast to the students a daily television segment that includes three minutes of commercials for designer jeans, candy bars, and the like. School used to be the one safe haven from advertisers, but no longer.

3. School Performance

". . . The first people who understood television, at least in the United States, were the advertising community. They grasped its significance immediately. The second group in the United States who figured it out were the politicians, because they saw the consequence that television would have in campaigning, in reaching the electorate. The last group which is finally awakening from its slumber are the educators, the teachers. They finally are beginning to realize that television is a monumental change in the way people think, in the way people spend their time."

—Newton Minow, former Federal
Communications Commission chairman

Early studies, which failed to control for IQ and socio-economic status, showed variable effects of heavy viewing on school performance. More recent, better-controlled studies have consistently found a significant harmful effect of more than one to two hours a day of TV viewing on academic performance, especially reading scores. This is probably because of TV's displacing schoolwork and reading for pleasure.

On the other hand, some studies have found that children from broken homes or poor neighborhoods may actually do better in school if they watch one to two hours of TV at home. TV may represent their only "window on the world."

4. Stereotyping

❑

"How a Woman Responds to Sax" (advertisement): A young man and woman are shown in three separate frames—meeting, touching, then kissing passionately. Pictured beneath them is a bottle of Saxon aftershave lotion. The caption reads, "Even if it's the first time, most women love Sax. Of course, you can't base a relationship on Sax. But it can make a difference. Discover the Joy of Sax."

❑

We sixties children want a better world for our kids. We grew up in the era of civil rights marches and race riots, antiwar protests, feminism and bra-burnings. During part of our childhood, in the South you couldn't be black and eat at white restaurants, go to white schools, or even drink from white water fountains. Women have progressed from being "happy homemakers" to being senators, mayors, governors, even a Supreme Court Justice. Yet children's television is still completely dominated by white male figures, who are 75 to 90 percent of all characters. Children's cartoons are particularly rich in stereotypes, with villains usually possessing non-Caucasian features and speaking in foreign accents. Most villains attack an all-American hero figure and therefore may promote an "us versus them" attitude.

For adolescents who are trying to figure out their place in the adult world, the TV world is overpopulated with doctors, lawyers, and policemen, giving the mistaken impression that only professionals have value in adult society. By contrast, old people are underrepresented on American television and are frequently shown as feeble grandparents bearing cookies. A 1988 report found that teenage girls are also stereotypically portrayed: obsessed with shopping and boys; incapable of having serious conversations about academic interests or career goals; convinced that their looks are far more important than their brains.

Television may have many more-subtle effects as well. The sixties and seventies were the starting point for the feminist movement, and many of you may sympathize (as I do) with much of its philosophy. So you may be dismayed to learn that young children who watch twenty-five hours or more of television a week demonstrate more stereotypical sex-role attitudes than those who watch ten hours or less a week. Several studies have shown that television encourages such notions as "women are happiest at home raising children" and "men are born with more ambition than women." As the 1982 report on TV by the National Institutes of Mental Health concluded, the single most significant aspect of a child's learning about human sexuality is the set of messages that relate to "normal" male and female characteristics and roles in life. Although American television has made some progress in this area, even the independent women now depicted in prime-time programming frequently depend on men for advice and direction, lose control more often than men, and become more emotionally involved.

5. Prosocial Television

> "Children are demanding. They are the most attentive, congenial readers on earth. They accept, almost without question, anything you present them with, as long as it is presented honestly, fearlessly, and clearly. . . . Anybody who writes down to children is simply wasting his time. You have to write up, not down."
>
> —E. B. WHITE, the author of
> Charlotte's Web

Television can be a powerful prosocial teacher of children and adolescents. As *Sesame Street* and *Mister Rogers' Neighborhood* have demonstrated, children can learn many valuable ideas about racial harmony, cooperation, and kindness, as well as simple arithmetic and the alphabet. For preteens and teenagers, shows like *Degrassi Junior High*, *Degrassi High*, *Roseanne*, *I'll Fly Away*, and *Beverly Hills 90210* have dealt sensitively with such controversial subjects as AIDS, alcoholism, racism, teen pregnancy, and drugs. One of the best things about television is that it can take us where we may never be able to go (exotic places, outer space), show us people worthy of emulating, keep us informed about world events, and—yes—even entertain us. The tragedy of American television is that occasionally it can be so good (for example, Richard

Attenborough's *Life on Earth* series, Ken Burns's *Civil War*), and yet typically it is so bad. Imagine if, every time your preteens or teenagers turned on the TV set, they could choose from among an afternoon special, a nature special, a storybook theater presentation, a showing of the *Black Stallion* movie, and episodes of *I'll Fly Away, Beverly Hills 90210*, and *The Wonder Years*.

6. Obesity and Eating Disorders

> *"Television presents viewers with two sets of conflicting messages. One suggests that we eat in ways almost guaranteed to make us fat; the other suggests that we strive to remain slim."*
>
> —TV researcher
> LOIS KAUFMAN

Recent evidence points to heavy TV viewing as one direct cause of obesity in children and adolescents. This may be because watching TV is such a passive activity, because many unhealthy products are advertised, such as sugar-coated cereals and junk food, or because many people tend to snack while viewing television. In the past several years I have seen numerous children and adolescents whose parents were worried that they were overweight or frankly obese. My first question to these families is "How much TV does your child watch?" The usual response is "Four or five hours a day," even for teenagers. If even one of those hours were spent in vigorous physical activity, there probably wouldn't be a problem to discuss. There are even some preliminary data to suggest that when children watch television, they burn less calories than when they're sleeping! I think that someone could make a fortune by developing a device that connected an exercise bicycle to the TV set; the set would stay on only as long as the viewer was pedaling hard enough.

Television may also contribute to the development of such serious eating disorders as anorexia nervosa and bulimia. Studies show that TV characters are usually happy in the presence of food, yet food is rarely consumed to satisfy hunger. Rather, it is used to bribe others or to facilitate social interactions—precisely some of the dynamics involved in anorexia nervosa. Like other media, television has an obsession with thin people: Eighty-eight percent of all characters are thin or average in body build, and obese people are usually subjected to ridicule. Several recent surveys of adolescents have found that both males and females are extremely fearful of being obese, even when they are actually underweight. Aside from the portrayal of Roseanne and Dan in *Roseanne* as being both overweight and hip and in control, the one other attempt to buck this trend was the British Broadcasting Corporation's 1985 ban on televising beauty pageants, calling them "an anachronism in this day and age of equality, and verging on the offensive."

7. Sex and Sexuality

"[Teenagers], if they've watched **Dallas**, already have a working familiarity with lust. They learned about impotence from **Donahue**. Love, Sidney taught them about homosexuality, and, one hopes, tolerance. Kojak told them all about the street names for prostitution and prostitutes. Soap operas offer daily classes in frigidity, menopause, abortion, infidelity and loss of appetite. If they've watched more than one made-for-television movie, they know about rape. Johnny Carson gives graduate courses in divorce and Jerry Falwell has already spoiled all of it with his class—"An

Overview of Sin 101." Parents should probably view tele-
vision as a blessing; after all, it took television to finally get
sex education out of the schools and back in the home, where
it belongs. Call it educational TV."

—LINDA ELLERBEE,
And So It Goes—
Adventures in Television

Because we parents do such a poor job of sex education
at home, and because school-based programs are often
inadequate or offered too late, television fills the void. Sex
is used to sell everything from shampoo to cars, yet birth
control advertising remains taboo on national network
TV. Worse yet, this is occurring despite the fact that every
poll ever taken on the subject documents that the majority
of Americans would like to see more responsible sexuality
in programming and would approve of contraceptive advertisements' being aired. Consider the following public
service announcement (PSA), produced in 1985 by the
American College of Obstetricians and Gynecologists:

"I Intend"

A bright young black woman speaks to the camera: "I
intend to be President."

A bright young white woman speaks to the camera: "I
intend to go to college."

A third young woman, obviously pregnant, confesses:
"I intended to start a family. But not this soon."

Announcer: "Nothing changes any intentions faster
than an unintended pregnancy. Unintended pregnancies
have risks, greater risks than any of today's contraceptives.
The American College of Obstetricians and Gynecologists
wants you to have the facts. For your free booklet call
1-800-I-INTENDS."

A fourth young woman: "I intend to call, now."

This public service announcement continues to be banned by the national networks. Why? As a vice-president of one of the major networks explained, "The 'I Intend' PSAs are not suitable for broadcast because people might get offended, and that could end up costing us a lot of viewers, and therefore a lot of money." I told him that lots of people were already offended—by soap operas, talk shows, and prime-time shows that flaunt irresponsible sexuality. He answered that people might be offended, but such shows make lots of money because people still watch them. He did volunteer that the major networks might be willing to air the "I Intend" PSA if the offensive line were removed. I asked him which line he was referring to. He said it was "Unintended pregnancies have risks, greater risks than any of today's contraceptives."

American television is the sexiest, the most exploitive, the least responsible in the world. The networks, producers, and advertisers will use *anything* to sell a program or a product. For example, in 1989 CBS launched a new sitcom entitled *Live In*, about a New Jersey family that imports an Australian au pair girl. Tom Shales, a prominent TV critic, reviewed the show this way:

> By an unwritten law of television, domestic sitcoms must have a randy, hyperglandular teen-age boy in the house. In this case, the kid's name is Danny. . . . When Danny is not salivating or making suggestive remarks, a moronic friend called Gator does it for him.
>
> "So, did you boff her yet?" Gator asked on the first show. When Danny said he hadn't made it to first base, Gator scoffed, "The chick is obviously frigid." Seeing Lisa "naked" then became the project *du jour*; the boys drilled a hole in a wall so they could watch her undress.
>
> As irony will have it, Lisa looked through the hole and saw Danny naked instead. Later, she made mocking ref-

erence to his genitals, summoning the image of a baby carrot and remarking, "Immature things are usually small." This was in front of the rest of the family at the dinner table.

Good clean fun? Or pandering puerile pap?

—*ALBUQUERQUE JOURNAL*,
March 23, 1989

Since *Live-In* was later canceled, you may think that I am making too big an issue out of this. But consider the fact that the show aired at 8 P.M. (EDT) and was viewed in approximately *12.6 million* American households (Nielsen ratings, March 29, 1989). There should be no doubt in anyone's mind about how powerful television is as a medium, and how effectively it can teach children and adolescents. It's also interesting that for years network executives claimed that they were simply giving the American public what it wanted—sex and violence. Yet in the 1980s, along came the number-one-rated hits *Family Ties* and *The Cosby Show*, neither of which had any illicit sex or violence—and somehow the network executives didn't get the message. They claimed that both shows were simply "aberrations."

Since teenage sex is such an important topic with parents, let's take a close look at what's on TV and how it might be influencing teenagers. If you simply count up what's on American TV, here's what you get: Americans view more than twenty-seven instances an hour of sexual behavior on television. Annually, the networks broadcast approximately 65,000 sexual references during the afternoon and prime-time periods alone. Based on Nielsen data on the amount of television watched, this means that American children and adolescents view nearly 14,000 sexual references a year. Of these, only 165 refer to such topics as abstinence, sex education, birth control, or self-control. That represents a ratio of about one to eighty-five. Looking at the trends over the past thirteen years, explicitness is rapidly replacing suggestiveness. Explicit portrayal of sexual intercourse occurred for the first time during the 1987–88 TV season, and the number of verbal references to intercourse has risen dramatically, now averaging over one an hour.

Most intelligent adults would agree that soap operas represent the most sensational and unrealistic view of normal adult sexuality. Unfortunately, soap operas are extremely popular among teenagers and preteens, especially girls. Kids see their favorite soap stars as role models. And there is even a study which found that teenagers who become pregnant watch more soap operas, are more likely to believe that their favorite soap opera characters wouldn't use birth control, and think that soap operas portray real adult relationships.

Our kids are surrounded by cues that say to them, "Sex is fun, sex is sexy, sex has no risks associated with it, and everybody is doing it, so why not you?" Nowhere is there a mention of getting pregnant, or contracting a sexually transmitted disease, or abstinence. The 1985 Guttmacher Report, which discovered that the United States has the highest teenage pregnancy rate of thirty-seven developed countries, had this to say about American media and sex:

American teenagers seem to have inherited the worst of all possible worlds regarding their exposure to messages about sex: Movies, music, radio and TV tell them that sex is romantic, exciting, titillating: premarital sex and cohabitation are visible ways of life among adults they see and hear about. . . . Yet, at the same time, young people get the message good girls should say no. Almost nothing they see or hear about sex informs them about contraception or the importance of avoiding pregnancy.

Clearly, we can't have it both ways. Do I think that we should eliminate all sexual references from TV and the media? Certainly not. Am I just being prudish? I don't think so. Sex is an integral part of human life and can be portrayed intelligently and appropriately. I simply think that it is unfair to young people to portray sex the way we do in the media and then expect them to be perfect little ladies and gentlemen until they are married. It is equally unfair for teenagers to have to learn about sex through the media, rather than at school, in church, or at home. And finally, it is wrong to dangle sex in front of teenagers the way we do and not give them access to the one product that could prevent a tragedy—birth control.

How *should* sex be portrayed in the media? Here are some suggested guidelines for the media that were developed by the Center for Population Options:

- Recognize sex as a healthy and natural part of life.
- Parent and child conversations about sex are important and healthy and should be encouraged.
- Demonstrate that not only the young, unmarried, and beautiful have sexual relationships.
- Not all affection and touching must culminate in sex.
- Portray couples having sexual relationships with feelings of affection, love, and respect for one another.
- Consequences of unprotected sex should be discussed or shown.
- Miscarriage should not be used as a dramatic convenience for resolving an unwanted pregnancy.
- Use of contraceptives should be indicated as a normal part of a sexual relationship.

- Avoid associating violence with sex or love.
- Rape should be depicted as a crime of violence, not of passion.
- The ability to say "no" should be recognized and respected.

Now that we know how sexy American TV is, how much do we know about such programming's actual effect on kids? The answer is, a lot. Many studies attest to television's ability to transmit information and shape attitudes. It gives viewers, especially children, a sense of what normal social behavior is. Remember that young adolescents' identities are just jelling and are still malleable; meanwhile, TV gives them their first glimpse into the secretive world of adult sex before they can learn from their own, firsthand experience. Because of their inexperience, teenagers may be especially vulnerable to a "Sexy World Syndrome" if they have grown up watching a lot of TV. One of the primary messages from the soaps and prime-time shows is that adults do not talk about or use contraception and, in fact, don't plan to have sex at all. Being "swept away" is the natural way to have sex. Funny thing: That's exactly how most adolescent females think, too. In several studies, female teens who failed to contracept gave "sex just happened" and "there was no time to prepare" as their leading reasons.

Not all TV shows depict human sexuality in a bad light. Shows like *Degrassi Junior High*, *Growing Pains*, *Roseanne*, *Beverly Hills 90210*, a variety of afternoon specials, and made-for-TV movies like *Babies Having Babies* and *Daddy* have responsibly handled the issue of teenage sexual activity and pregnancy. *Cagney and Lacey* was one of the first instances of a TV mother talking to her son about responsibility and birth control. And during the 1987–88 season prime-time TV's first mention of using a diaphragm occurred, on an episode of *St. Elsewhere* (its user was the Chief of Obstetrics and Gynecology).

In the past two TV seasons the threat of AIDS has loosened things up just a bit on prime-time TV, but network censors still insist that any discussion of condoms be linked to the prevention of AIDS but not to the prevention of other STDs or of pregnancy. It also seems a shame that it took a deadly virus to begin accomplishing what one million teenage pregnancies a year couldn't do.

8. Alcohol and Cigarettes

> *"You don't see dead teenagers on the highway because of corn chips."*
>
> —JAY LENO, on why he does
> commercials for corn chips
> but refuses to do beer ads

> *"I was actually in treatment in Minnesota when that came on the TV. I was in a room full of recovering alcoholics, myself being one of them, and everybody went, 'Is that you?' "*
>
> —ERIC CLAPTON,
> on his beer commercial

It is sadly ironic that American networks refuse to allow advertising for a product (contraceptives) that would prevent untold numbers of pregnancies and STDs, yet gladly accept advertising for a product (alcohol) that is involved in 25 to 50 percent of all adolescent deaths. Unquestionably, there is a link between advertising and increased consumption of product; otherwise, why would beer and wine manufacturers spend $900 million a year on advertising? That is far too high a price tag to "influence brand choice," which is what advertisers say their commercials are limited to doing. Since 1960, per capita consumption of alcohol in the United States has increased 50 percent. In Sweden, per capita consumption of alcohol dropped 20 percent when ads were banned.

But Hollywood can be socially responsible, too. In 1983 the Hollywood Caucus of Producers, Writers, and Directors issued guidelines for the industry, suggesting that programs avoid gratuitous alcohol use, glamorizing drinking, or showing drinking with no serious consequences or as a macho activity. More recently, the Harvard Alcohol Project has joined with the major TV networks and studios to develop programming aimed at attacking the specific problem of drinking and driving. Unfortunately, the problem of beer and wine advertising remains. Although manufacturers are now devising "know when to say when" campaigns, this has been primarily in response to the threat of a complete ban on all TV beer and wine ads. In addition, for every such public service announcement teenagers see, they will see twenty-five to fifty ads in which the implicit messages are: Beer is fun, people who drink beer have more fun and are more successful in life, and "real" men drink beer.

Hollywood has also changed the depiction of cigarette smoking. In the 1960s TV doctors like Ben Casey, Dr. Kildare, and Dr. Gillespie all smoked. Now doctors are never portrayed as smokers, and only 2 percent of series stars smoke. In movies, however, smoking seems to be making a comeback. More than 80 percent of current films contain tobacco use. Everyone knows that cigarette advertising has been banned from TV. What most people don't realize is that this hasn't stopped tobacco companies from advertising their products—to the tune of more than $6 billion a year—more than any other product in the United States. Print-media ads, billboards, and sponsorship of motor rac-

ing, women's tennis, and other sports events have allowed tobacco companies to circumvent the television ban
on advertising. The Philip Morris Company reportedly
paid $350,000 to place Lark cigarettes in *License to Kill*, a
James Bond film, and $42,500 to place Marlboros in *Super-
man II*.

It seems a shame that although we all want the best for
our children, we constantly have to battle the forces of big
business and commercialism to achieve it.

9. Homicide and Suicide

> *It's not enough to say that Shakespeare and Marlowe were
> violent and civilization still survived. Technology has
> brought a new amplification into play. Never before has so
> much violence been shown so graphically to so many.*
>
> —J. MORGENSTERN
> (*Newsweek*, 1972)

> *"I'm glad this boy never read Shakespeare in school, because
> he would have shot himself years earlier."*
>
> —SINGER OZZY OSBORNE'S WIFE, commenting
> on the lawsuit brought by the parents of a
> nineteen-year-old male who committed
> suicide after listening to Osborne's song
> "Suicide Solution"

America has a love affair with guns, and the flirtation
is frequently played out on prime-time television shows
and in the movies. Guns are glorified in such cartoon
shows as *G.I. Joe, He-Man and Masters of the Universe*, and
Rambo, and in prime-time shows like *Top Cops* and detective series that are popular with older children and teen-

agers. Weapons appear an average of nine times an hour in prime-time TV shows. And body counts have risen steadily in such recent popular movies as *Terminator 2*, *Batman*, *RoboCop 2*, *Die Hard 2*, *Total Recall*, and *Lethal Weapon 3*. At the same time, the United States leads the Western world in both handgun availability and handgun deaths. Violence in American society has steadily increased as the depiction of violence on TV and movie screens has become more graphic. Is this cause and effect or coincidence? The research indicates that this is *not* coincidental.

Homicide and suicide are the second and third leading causes of death among teenagers, and guns contribute to both in a major way. This is *not* about the U.S. Constitution or the National Rifle Association. It's about public health—specifically, your family's health. In 1992 the American Academy of Pediatrics—which represents forty-five thousand pediatricians in the United States and Latin America—called for a ban on handguns, air guns, and assault weapons. American children are more likely to be shot than children in any other country, and guns kept at home are forty-three times as likely to kill a family member as a criminal intruder. Each year the United States has more than 10,000 handgun homicides, compared to 52 or fewer in other developed countries. In addition, there are more than 150,000 nonfatal firearm injuries a year. Even toy guns are responsible for 1,500 injuries a year to children and adolescents, and the sale of toy guns is a nearly $100 million industry.

Numerous studies now link television or newspaper publicity about suicide with an increase in teenage suicide. Although the mechanism of this effect is unknown, role modeling probably plays a significant role. During the past three decades—interestingly, the "golden age of TV violence"—the suicide rate among teens has tripled, and suicide now accounts for 8 percent of all deaths in late adolescence. Given the frequency of suicidal thoughts among teenagers, and the fact that suicide gestures out-number successful attempts by 100–200 to 1, allowing teenagers access to firearms in the home and glamorizing guns on TV seems especially foolish.

10. Rock Music and Music Videos

"I'm gonna force you at gun point to eat me alive . . . squealing in passion as the rod steel injects."

> —"Eat Me Alive" by JUDAS
> PRIEST (from *Defenders of the Faith*, Columbia Records,
> 2 million copies sold)

"Manipulation of children's minds in the field of religion or politics would touch off a parental storm and a rash of Congressional investigations. But in the world of commerce, children are fair game and legitimate prey."

> —Liner notes from the album *Welcome to the Pleasure Dome* by the rock group FRANKIE
> GOES TO HOLLYWOOD

"Sex sells in America, and as the advertising world has grown ever more risqué in pushing cars, cosmetics, jeans, and liquor to adults, pop music has been forced further past the fringes of respectability for its rebellious thrills. When Mom and Dad watch a Brut commercial in which a nude woman puts on her husband's shirt and sensuously rubs his after-shave all over herself, well, what can a young boy do? Play in a rock 'n' roll band and be a bit more outrageous than his parents want him to be. Kids' natural anti-authoritarianism is going to drive them to the frontiers of sexual fantasy in a society where most

aspects of the dirty deed have been appropriated by racy advertising and titillating TV cheesecakery."

—TERENCE MORAN
(*The New Republic*,
August 12–19, 1985)

When Little Richard recorded "Good golly, Miss Molly/ Sure likes to bawl" in 1959, he was not singing about a young woman with a blocked tear duct; nor was the Rolling Stones' 1960s hit "Let's Spend the Night Together" about a vacationing family planning to stay all in one room in a Motel-6. Of course, Jimmy Rodgers' 1930s lyrics, like "And if you don't wanna smell my smoke/Don't monkey with my gun," were not exactly pristine either. Many American songwriters and singers in the twentieth century have seemed obsessed with seeing how much they can get away with. And adult society has usually responded with concern and even outrage. But the outcry over lyrics has not been confined to the last two or three decades. Cole Porter's "The Lady Is a Tramp" is not the theme song from the Walt Disney movie, nor is his "Let's Do It" about a couple deciding to play scrabble. The difference is that where Cole Porter was wittily evasive, current rock stars like Prince clearly define what "it" is.

Nothing angers many parents today more than sexy, violent, or satanic rock music lyrics. Yet rock 'n' roll music has always been antiestablishment and provocative, and *must continue to be*—it serves as an important badge of adolescence. Of all people, we should be able to understand that. Ours was the first generation of teenagers to grow up with rock 'n' roll. Our parents were the ones who shook their heads when they saw Elvis Presley gyrate his pelvis and couldn't understand why we idolized the Beatles and the Rolling Stones. It all sounded like just so much noise to them. We should be capable of far more tolerance. But just how far should our tolerance go? It is unfortunately true that rock music lyrics have become far more provocative than when we were growing up. Consider these lyrics:

> Gonna blow you to a million pieces,
> Blow you sky high . . .
> Splatter matter on the bloody ceiling . . .
> Gotta get into a fight.
>
>>   —"Fight" by the
>>   ROLLING STONES
>>   (from *Dirty Work*,
>>   Columbia Records)

> I knew a girl named Nikki
> I guess you could say she was a sex fiend.
> I met her in a hotel lobby
> Masturbating with a magazine.
>
>>   —"Darling Nikki" by
>>   PRINCE (from *Purple*
>>   *Rain*, Warner
>>   Records, 9 million
>>   copies sold,
>>   Grammy Award–
>>   winner)

> Don't you struggle
> Don't you fight
> Let me put my love into you
> Let me cut your cake with my knife.
>
>>   —"Let Me Put My
>>   Love into You" by
>>   AC/DC (from *Back in*
>>   *Black*, Atlantic
>>   Records)

> She don't like other women
> She likes whips and chains
> She likes cocaine
> And flippin' out with Great Danes. . . .
>
> —"Under Pressure" by
> ZZ Top (from
> *Eliminator*, Warner
> Bros. Records,
> platinum LP)

While sexually suggestive, drug-oriented, violent, or satanic lyrics serve no useful purpose, neither have they been shown to have any adverse behavioral effects. In fact, conservative groups' attempts to label record albums and publicize lyrics on record jackets may be actually be counterproductive, according to what little research exists in this area:

- Only 30 percent of teenagers seem to know the lyrics to their favorite songs (40 percent if they are heavy metal fans).
- Even if they know the lyrics, older children and younger adolescents may not comprehend their meaning. For example, only 10 percent of fourth-graders in one study could correctly interpret Madonna's "Like a Virgin." Comprehension increases with age, but nearly half of college students studied by one researcher mistakenly thought that Bruce Springsteen's hit "Born in the USA" was a song of patriotism, not alienation.
- Teenagers' motivation, knowledge, and experience are crucial factors in their ability to interpret lyrics. They frequently miss the sexual themes in lyrics and interpret their favorite songs in terms of "love, friendship, growing up" rather than the sex, violence, and

satanism that adults see in them. Consequently, publicizing lyrics may make them *more* accessible to teenagers. Likewise, putting ratings on record albums may simply advertise their antiauthority appeal for teens.

Perhaps the only significant behavioral finding has been that heavy metal music, which lies at the outer limits of rock 'n' roll, may serve as a useful marker for depressed or disturbed adolescents. Given the present lack of incriminating evidence, the wisest stance seems to be benign tolerance, combined with a strong anticensorship position, and perhaps a prayer to the music industry to exercise voluntary restraint and good taste. There are only two possible exceptions to this. One is heavy metal music, and here again, the entire gestalt of the adolescent is important. If he is a good student, seems to have many trustworthy friends, and is not overly combative at home, his taste for heavy metal music can probably be dismissed. If, on the other hand, he keeps his bedroom door locked, barely says two words a week to you, is suspended from school, and comes in at all hours of the night, then his affection for heavy metal music may be the least of your problems.

The other exception is the kind of antifemale rap music typified by 2 Live Crew. Consider these lyrics from *As Nasty As They Wanna Be* (Luke Sky):

> To have her walkin' funny we try to abuse it
> A big stinking pussy can't do it all
> So we try real hard just to bust the walls.

Although even this extremely offensive speech is arguably protected by the First Amendment, one would think that there would be such a hue and cry about such lyrics that no one would dare to record them. And certainly the fact such lyrics are protected constitutionally does not mean that you, as parents, can't ban them from your household. Busting women's vaginas, calling women bitches, forcing oral sex—this sort of music may have to be tolerated reluctantly by a freedom-loving society, but it certainly does not have to be condoned.

In the past five years a number of conservative groups and a few state legislatures have pushed for labeling of record albums. Currently, the music industry has agreed to the following voluntary label: "Explicit Lyrics—Parental Advisory." We might as well be waving a red flag in front of teenagers, leading them to the forbidden fruit. Given what we know about how few kids really comprehend the lyrics of the songs they are listening to, labeling seems to be a misguided idea, and publicizing lyrics may make them more accessible to children and teens who otherwise would not know or understand them. Remember "Louie Louie" by the Kingsmen? The Federal Communications Commission played it forward and backward, at 33, 45, and 78 rpm, and still couldn't figure out what the lyrics were. They concluded: "The song is unintelligible at any speed." Imagine if we simply could have read the album cover to find out what the lyrics really were!

Music videos are an entirely different story. Here's an example of how old we are getting—we are now able to use those famous words that our parents always used on us, "When I was young, we didn't have . . ." Music videos didn't exist when we were growing up. And unless you watch a lot of Music Television (MTV), you may have no idea of what they are or what they contain. Are music videos more akin to music and radio or to television? And does that affect their impact on adolescents' attitudes and behavior? Although limited data are available, music videos clearly belong in the category of television. Teenagers may not hear or understand rock lyrics, but they cannot help but see the provocative and often violent images in music videos, particularly when their favorite rock stars are in them. In addition, MTV seems to appeal to adolescents who are not ordinarily heavy consumers of television. In one study of more than nine hundred San Jose teens, those with access to MTV watched an average of up to two hours per day.

Although it is not quite synonymous with music videos, MTV is clearly the most significant music video medium. Occasionally the networks show music videos late at night, but these shows don't have as large an audience as MTV does and present far tamer videos. MTV, begun in 1981, reaches 40 percent of all U.S. households (thirty-five million subscribers), and by 1987 it had begun generating approximately $60 million in annual revenues. It claims to have a weekly "penetration" of half the U.S. adolescent market—an amusing Freudian slip, since MTV commercially exploits teenagers (the way Saturday-morning TV exploits younger children) without giving them much in return.

Many of us probably look at MTV the way our parents looked at *American Bandstand*. On one episode of *The Cosby Show*, Cliff Huxtable insists that his son Theo turn off MTV and refers to music videos as "nightmares set to music." The creator of MTV, Robert Pittman, initially hailed it as "a new art form." There is no question that it has had a major impact on American culture. The real question is, has that impact been good or bad?

MTV can be divided into three different parts: performance videos, concept videos, and advertising. Performance videos basically show the various bands playing their songs. Rock stars' onstage antics have intensified considerably since Elvis Presley, and so you can witness the lead singer of Aerosmith humping his microphone, or David Lee Roth masturbating with a huge inflatable phallus. All of this seems more consciously provocative than actually harmful and probably does not represent a significant problem. On the other hand, concept videos tell a story, and that *can* be problematic. In one study, more than half of all concept videos involved violence, three-quarters involved sex, and often the two were combined, with women the usual targets. Looking at MTV is like looking through a time tunnel into the 1950s. It is the single most male-chauvinistic entertainment medium short of pornography. Concept videos are strongly male-oriented, half of all the women depicted are provocatively dressed, and women are frequently worshipped as upper-class sex goddesses (Billy Joel's "Uptown Girl," ZZ Top's "Legs," the Thunderbirds' "Wrap It Up"). Rock stars also serve as role models for impressionable teens and pre-teens. When Madonna sings "Papa don't preach/I'm in trouble deep/Papa don't preach/I've been losing sleep/But I made up my mind/I'm keeping my baby" while dancing around looking like a thin Marilyn Monroe, it becomes that much more difficult to persuade a pregnant fourteen-year-old that having a baby will be a severe hardship. George Michael's "I Want Your Sex" combines striking sexual imagery with explicit lyrics ("Sex is natural/Sex is good/Not everybody does it/ But everybody should") with a disclaimer: "This song is not about casual sex. . . . Explore Monogamy." If tobacco manufacturers tried an analogous ploy with cigarette labeling, the disclaimer might read: "Caution: Cigarettes may be hazardous to your health, but only if you smoke them."

Advertising on MTV parallels prime-time advertising in that sex is used to sell everything but the one product that teenagers could really benefit from—birth control. Occasionally there are public service announcements about AIDS, some of which even mention condoms. Alcohol ads are abundant on MTV, which seems peculiar if the target audience is really meant to be teenagers.

Few behavioral studies exist regarding music videos or MTV. One study demonstrated that viewing violent videos may desensitize young people to violence. Another found that music videos are self-reinforcing: If viewers hear a song after having seen the video version, they immediately "flash back" to the visual imagery in the video. MTV has also revolutionalized other forms of visual media. Commercials are more rapid-fire, as are movies. Some critics have complained that the *Sesame Street* generation has grown up into the MTV generation.

Not all of MTV is bad or even potentially harmful. Perhaps 5 to 10 percent of the videos are extremely creative and interesting to watch: Peter Gabriel's "Sledgehammer" and Dire Straits' "Money for Nothing" are examples of the new visual imagery; M.C. Hammer's "U Can't Touch This" makes you want to get up and dance; and Quiet Riot's "The Young and the Free" is a parody that could serve as an anthem for this generation's love of rock 'n' roll without restraints. Certain videos even have prosocial themes: for example, Janet Jackson's "You Don't Have to Take Your Clothes Off to Have Fun" and "This One's for You," Neil Young's indictment of beer advertisers. But, as is true of the other networks, MTV contains more bad than good programming, more unhealthful than healthful content. This is a pity, since MTV has a unique ability to reach American teenagers. Contraceptive advertising would seem a natural for MTV. On the other hand, beer and wine ads are dreadfully out of place on it and typify the network's primary goal of making money, no matter what the cost.

OTHER MEDIA

"What television suggests, the films do."

—TV researcher
BRADLEY GREENBERG

This chapter has focused primarily on television, because it is the single most important medium in people's lives, in terms of both time spent watching and the effectiveness of TV as a teacher. But older children and teenagers spend time with other media as well, and before we discuss what sort of damage-control strategies you should be using to try to offset the influence of the media on your kids, we should examine the known effects of movies, radio, and pornography.

Movies. The movies are less significant than TV only because they consume much less time and are usually viewed with friends, thus allowing socializing influences to temper whatever potential harmful effects exist. If teenagers see two movies a week at their local cinema, that represents only 10 to 15 percent of the time that they spend watching TV in an average week. This does not mean that movies are insignificant, however. Many of us still remember the death of Bambi's mother or the shower scene in *Psycho.* Seventy-five percent of American households with children now have a videocassette recorder, and video stores do not seem particularly interested in enforcing the "R" rating (nor do theater owners). In one survey of fifteen- to sixteen-year-olds in three Michigan cities, more than half had seen the most recent popular R-rated movies, either in a movie theater or on a VCR at home.

Compared with television, movies have a frequency of

sexual references and acts that is seven times as high and much franker. Studies of movies in the past few decades show that sex is for the young, is an "action activity," and, as on TV, is rarely accompanied by any discussion of birth control. As discussed previously, movies have also grown increasingly violent, including sexual violence, and portray the use of such drugs a cocaine and heroin, which are rarely seen on TV.

During the past two decades Hollywood has increasingly pandered to teenagers because of the demographics of the business: Adolescents are the largest moviegoing segment of the population. Unfortunately, this not only decreases the number of films available to the rest of us, it also frequently insults the intelligence of American teenagers. Not every teenager is interested in exploitive portrayals of teenage sex (*Porky's I, II,* and *III,* for example) or of teenagers in general (any John Hughes movie). And certainly the rash of "slice and dice" movies cannot exactly be beneficial to teenagers' conception of women and violence (for examples, see the *Halloween, Nightmare on Elm Street,* and *Friday the 13th* series). Teenagers and older children may be learning that acting aggressively toward women is normal and expected in adult society.

The occasional good children's or adolescents' movie seems to be lost in the crowd of overly violent or sexy films that gather all the attention and revenues. But some films are worth mentioning for their "kinder and gentler" view of childhood and adolescence: *My Life as a Dog, Breaking Away, Hope and Glory, Salaam Bombay, The Wizard of Loneliness, Fanny and Alexander, The Little Mermaid, My Bodyguard, Cinema Paradiso, The Black Stallion, Small Change, Au Revoir les Enfants, Dead Poets' Society, Big, Harold and Maude, My Father's Glory, My Mother's Castle,* and *Stand By Me.* Other films, with a harder edge, at least have contributed some new insights into contemporary adolescence: *River's Edge, Pump Up the Volume, The Outsiders, Streetwise, The Tin Drum, Boyz 'n the Hood, Ramblin' Rose,* and *Heathers.*

Radio. Although teenagers spend a lot of time with the radio on as a background accompaniment to doing homework, driving, or talking with friends, its importance is probably overrated. Teens average 3.7 hours listening to the radio on weekdays and 6.4 hours on weekends, but much of this time is not active listening. According to the limited research that has been done, when teenagers claim that they are just listening to the beat, not the lyrics, they are probably telling the truth.

Pornography. There is no more controversial topic in the media than the effect of pornography on behavior. Even the definitions vary widely, from Supreme Court Justice Potter Stewart's "I know it when I see it" to Senator Jesse Helms's views on modern art. If you want the scientific word on the subject, the research seems to indicate that pornography that is sexually explicit but not violent carries little risk. However, violent pornography could lead to an increase in aggression, and some researchers feel that even nonviolent pornography can lead to significant changes in men's attitudes about women.

If you have a teenage son, your biggest defense against pornography is taking away the curiosity factor. If, for example, he saw you and your spouse naked as he was growing up, and the two of you treated it very matter-of-factly, chances are that he won't need to seek out *Hustler* to see what an adult woman looks like. As always, you are his crucial role models. If Dad keeps a copy of *Penthouse* magazine by his bed, I'd bet the mortgage that Junior will read it, probably sooner rather than later. If Dad ogles women at the beach, or makes suggestive comments to female friends, or prides himself on telling dirty jokes, Junior will certainly get the message. To me, a copy of *Playboy* under Junior's bed when he's thirteen is more a sign of Junior's natural curiosity and of failure on your part to educate him properly about sex than it is a sign of Junior's moral weakness.

WHAT TO DO?

> *"I believe television is going to be the test of the modern world, and that in this new opportunity to see beyond the range of our vision we shall discover either a new and unbearable disturbance of the general peace, or a soaring radiance in the sky."*
>
> —E.B. WHITE (1938)

> *"Until television has valuable interesting programs for children, parents can simply get rid of the set. This would prevent their children from being brutalized by violence and made passive by long hours of immobilized viewing."*
>
> —BENJAMIN SPOCK

> *"Sending a child to his or her room takes on a whole new meaning today if the child's room is linked to the outside world through television, radio, telephone and computer."*
>
> —JOSHUA MYEROWITZ,
> No Sense of Place (1985)

We TV Generation kids grew up with TV but, paradoxically, we may underestimate its effects on our kids. Why? Because we had kinder and gentler shows to watch when we were growing up. Don't misunderstand me here. I'm not saying that we should feed nothing but pablum to our kids. I think *The Simpsons* is brilliant television—a direct descendant of *Rocky and Bullwinkle*. You can challenge the establishment, or poke fun at it, without giving kids harmful messages. Bart Simpson is a mischievous kid, but he always has to pay for his mistakes, and his heart is basically in the right place. *Mister Rogers' Neighborhood* is every bit the equivalent of *Captain Kangaroo*. And we had no equivalent of the excellent *Sesame Street* for young children, or *Beverly Hills 90210*, *Degrassi High*, *Roseanne*, or *The Wonder Years* for preteens and teens. But we can still do much, much better. Considering that kids watching three to four hours of TV a day, we *have* to do much, much better.

How do we make some practical sense out of all of this information?

Early Limits

You can begin limiting the amount of time your kids spend watching TV to no more than an hour or two a day. Ideally, this should take place as soon as they are old enough to watch—usually, around age one! But you can also gradually phase in such restrictions even with your preteens or teens. Some communities have experimented with "no television" weeks or even months, the most famous experiment occurring in Farmington, Connecticut, in 1984. Teachers there reported less aggressive behavior on the playground, and families found that they were doing more together.

Exceptions can always be made for special programs. What limiting TV time means is that you will have to find alternative activities for your younger children—playing outside, going to the zoo, reading, etc. Better yet, as your children get older, *they* will have to find alternative activities to amuse *themselves*. Many American parents have assumed that their children should avoid boredom, and television is seen as one activity that helps them do this.

Yet these same parents want their children to become creative and self-reliant. Boredom is actually one of those conditions that help children to develop creativity and self-reliance; consequently, it may be better to let your child be bored than to let her watch TV! Children who grow up parked in front of a TV set for hours on end begin to learn that when they have some free time, that's where it should be spent. Likewise, children who grow up seeing their parents camped in front of the TV set every night get a similar message. Parents are often told that they should begin reading to their infants as early as six months of age. What they are not often told is that they also should read *in front of* their two- to five-year-olds if they want their children to grow up to be avid readers.

Where does the limit of one to two hours a day come from? Given the amount of daily educational programming currently available from the networks, one to two hours a day will more than exhaust all the possibilities. Perhaps this recommendation might be different if we lived in Britain or Japan, but we don't, and the current state of American programming for children couldn't be worse. Limiting TV time will also, inevitably, increase time spent playing, usually outside. That will minimize your child's risk of obesity and improve his cardiovascular fitness. After school appears to be a critical time to exert such controls, because 80 percent of kids cite television as an important after-school activity. Likewise, there should be a house rule: No TV until your homework is done. This rule should be inviolable. Many studies show that children prefer doing almost anything more active than watching TV *if they are given the choice and opportunity*. It's up to parents to give them the opportunities.

Knowing What's On

You also need to familiarize yourselves with what's on TV. Go ahead, sit down and watch an entire Saturday morning's worth of children's TV. I still can't do it all in one sitting, and I'm supposed to be an expert on the subject. Don't just send your kids in to watch the tube and allow them to play "channel roulette" with the remote control. You wouldn't let your nine-year-old read a Danielle Steel novel or go to an R-rated movie, so why should you let her watch whatever she wants to on television?

I used to advise parents never to use the TV as an electronic baby sitter, but now I must admit that I was being hopelessly naïve. So instead I tell parents that when they want to park their kids for an hour or two, at least rent or prerecord some tapes for them to watch. The argument that children denied certain programs at home will merely watch them at a friend's house holds little merit; you could say the same thing about denying teenagers alcohol at home, or the use of a bedroom for sexual activities. Children and teenagers must still incorporate their parents' standards into their own, evolving values system— assuming, of course, that such values are actually presented.

Substituting Your Values for TV's Values

The next bit of advice is even more difficult for most parents: Watch TV *with* your kids. Television illustrates a wealth of human experience. However, since television consists of visual material, children may not be able to process it appropriately. Discussing what you are both watching may help provide a frame of reference for your child and allow you to insert your own values. If you watch TV with your children and discuss the content of what you're watching, your kids will have to process your views, which *will take precedence over whatever other views are being presented*. For example, if you sit and watch a soap opera with your preteen daughter and discuss why the characters are doing what they are doing, it then becomes a positive educational experience, no matter how bad the content of the program is. The same goes for violence on TV, but only if you discuss it with your kids: Why did the "good guy" shoot the "bad guy"? Is violence always necessary? Is it always right so long as you're the "good guy"? Were there other ways to solve the problem? What would you have done in that situation? What do you think happened to the "bad guy's" family? There are some excellent materials available to help you with this sort of dialogue (see appendix I).

Given the current content of American TV, a certain amount of preimmunization is probably necessary for your children. And that puts us back into your bailiwick: educating your kids about sex, drugs, relationships with other people, etc. The better job you do with educating them, the less susceptible they will be to others' influence.

Teaching Media Literacy

Educational curricula do exist that teach kids how to watch television. These programs show kids how special effects are done, how commercials are made so that products look more appealing, how actors create their roles, and so on. The goal is to help kids realize that TV programs and advertising present a very unreal world. Certain curricula also deal specifically with violence and have been effective in helping kids understand the unreality of TV violence. These are not particularly expensive or time-consuming curricula, but they require that some interested parents and teachers shepherd them into the overall curriculum.

Consumer Reports has two excellent twenty-eight-minute videos, *Buy Me That* (Home Box Office Productions, 1990) and a sequel, *Buy Me That, Too* (1992), which are designed to teach kids about how commercials are made, especially ads for toys, and how such ads may not always be entirely accurate. You don't need to buy a videocassette or live in a school district that teaches media literacy to begin to teach your child about television commercialism, however. Start by trying to get him to predict what kind of commercials will accompany a certain show—for example, an NBA basketball game (beer, cars, sneakers), a soap opera (products for women), a children's cartoon (toys, cereals). Then try discussing why this association exists. Next, try to compare what he sees in a commercial with the product in real life—a toy, for example. Tape a toy commercial, then go to the toy store and see if there is any resemblance between what's in the ad and the actual product. Go back and look at the commercial again, and see if you can identify what techniques were used to make the toy seem more attractive (music, camera angles, etc.). Ask your child why he thinks there is a difference.

The same goes for movies. Try discussing why a movie ends a certain way. Hollywood studios are notorious for insisting that their films have happy endings, even if the plot doesn't always justify them. The bottom line is always money. If kids can be taught to see the commercialism that exists just behind the TV or movie screen, they may be more resistant to the lure of Teenage Mutant Ninja Turtle merchandising or $125 pump-up sneakers.

Similar approaches can be used to discuss issues in regular TV programming. Count the number of men and women in a program and discuss how their roles differ.

Watch how minorities are portrayed on a detective show. Discuss why two apparent strangers are hopping into bed together on a soap opera.

Media literacy is something that our parents never taught us but we *must* teach our children—for their good, and ours. I know that it adds to what you perceive as an already heavy burden that you have as a parent. But if kids are going to spend three to four hours a day learning from the TV set, it is imperative that we try to direct and control that learning. Yes, Hollywood and the networks would make our jobs a whole lot easier if they would produce better programming, and we should be working toward that, but we can't afford to wait for changes that may or may not occur. You've got allies—your school, your PTA, your pediatrician. The concern about what kids are watching is definitely warranted, and the time to start intervening is now!

Changing the Industry

Parents' jobs would be much easier if there were some good choices available on TV, other than on PBS. To accomplish this, we are all going to have to return to our sixties roots and become political activists again. The first step is to join your PTA and work with your pediatrician. They can keep you up-to-date about new programs and the efforts to improve educational programming for children.

The second step is to understand how television is controlled, because that, too, is a political process. Television is regulated, not by the Constitution, but by an act of Congress—the Federal Communications Act of 1934, which specifically states that *we*, the public, own the airwaves and that the networks are merely leasing them to produce programming in *our* best interests. Things have

changed a little since 1934! A TV station's license to broadcast is now worth millions of dollars. How much of that
profit is returned to the general public in the form of educational or high-quality programming?

Both the FCC and Congress have the power to regulate
what you see on TV. In 1970, for example, Congress
passed the Public Health Cigarette Smoking Act, which
banned all cigarette advertisements from television. Unfortunately, what constitutes the public's "best interests"
has been subject to controversy and political maneuvering
for decades. The FCC has shifted first one way, then the
other. In 1961 Newton Minow, the FCC's chairman, declared that television was "a vast wasteland" and urged
broadcasters to improve the quality of children's television
in particular. In 1984 the new FCC chairman declared that
television was no more subject to being regulated than
were other home appliances. This was done at the behest
of President Reagan, who began the process of "deregu-
lation." In 1988 President Reagan actually vetoed the first
Children's Television Act, which would have made minor
improvements in children's programming. What all of this
meant to the television industry was that none of the four
major commercial networks (ABC, CBS, NBC, Fox) felt
compelled to broadcast *any* daily educational programming for children. The last such show was *Captain Kangaroo*, which was canceled in the early 1980s.

In 1990 a new version of the Children's Television Act
became law, despite President Bush's refusal to sign it.
This Act limits the amount of advertising on children's
programming to no more than 10.5 minutes per hour on
weekends and 12 minutes per hour on weekdays—something most stations were already doing. But the most significant provision of the Act is that stations now have to
prove, when they apply for renewal of their licenses, that
they have produced programs that serve the educational

and informational needs of children under the age of twelve. Of course, the FCC can decide not to vigorously enforce this provision—and the composition of the FCC depends on the President.

A second potentially important bill for parents concerned about TV was passed during the 1990 session of Congress. Senator Paul Simon's TV Violence Act gives broadcasters a three-year exemption from antitrust legislation so that they can meet and discuss how to reduce the amount of violence on television. The networks vigorously opposed the bill, but it passed anyway.

Congress has also examined the issue of beer and wine advertising on TV. In 1985 a movement to ban all alcohol ads on TV was initiated by several public interest groups but failed, in large part because of the strength of the alcohol lobby. More recent efforts have focused on increasing the amount of public service announcement counteradvertising or beginning a push for legislation that would mandate that beer and wine ads could only show and discuss the qualities of their product, not what their product will do for people. In Britain, for example, cigarette ads in the print media are not allowed to show people smoking.

How do you get involved in what looks to be a complicated and distant political process? You can start by writing to the networks, the FCC, and your congressional representatives, particularly if there is relevant legislation pending. The networks estimate that one letter represents ten thousand people. Serving as a monitor of your local TV stations may be extremely useful as well, since they all will eventually have to apply for license renewal. You also may find that you have more power to effect change at the local level. After all, the station manger has to answer to the local community. Asking for specific educational programming for children during after-school hours could be one goal. Station managers have considerable autonomy in deciding what programming should occupy the "flexible," non-network slots.

Letters to writers and producers can also have some effect, particularly if you write when you see a *good* program, rather than writing to threaten to boycott the advertisers' products. Threats of mass boycotts, and actual attempts to institute them, do little more than draw attention to the program, which makes it more popular than before.

Changing Hollywood and the movie industry may be an even tougher assignment. When a single picture can cost $50 million or more, it is unlikely that average citizens can have much impact, except by voting with their feet and not going to see objectionable pictures. But action can be taken at a local level—insisting that movie theater owners and video store managers honor the "R" rating and turn away kids under the age of seventeen. Parents also should familiarize themselves with what the ratings mean. There can be a surprising amount of profanity and violence in even a PG-13 movie. Insisting that your kids not see certain movies, with certain ratings, is entirely within your parental prerogatives. Yes, they may sneak down the hall and see an objectionable film anyway, but at least they'll know that you disapprove. On the other hand, if you watch a particularly objectionable R-rated film with your fifteen-year-old daughter and then discuss it with her, the film is no longer "objectionable" in the same way. As with watching soap operas on TV, it becomes a positive educational experience, despite the negative material.

What to do about MTV is another issue entirely. If your teenager wants an hour of MTV to count as her one hour a day of television, fine. But before you agree to that, watch MTV with your daughter and point out what exactly you find objectionable. Likewise, I'm not sure that I'd be willing to make a big fuss over a teenager who wanted to spend his own hard-earned money on a heavy metal album. But I *would* be interested in why he likes a particular group, how he views that group's antics or sexism, and how he feels about particular lyrics. It could become the beginning of a very interesting dialogue between the two of you on a number of subjects.

I've spent a lot of time talking about the media because they are the single most important aspect of child and adolescent learning and development that most parents overlook. You worry about school, you worry about whom you can trust to baby-sit for your kids, but most of you don't worry about letting them watch whatever they want on TV. And if they happen to sneak into an R-rated movie at age fourteen, you don't get terribly upset about that either. Parents in the 1990s will need more savvy than this. If we fail to understand the media's influence over our children and adolescents, we may be exposing them to potential harm. On the other hand, if we guide our kids carefully and appropriately, we can minimize the media's impact and strengthen our relationship with them at the same time.

Chapter 6

Parenting in the 1990s

❑

I began this book by stating that it is not easy being a parent in the 1990s. It requires new skills and new strategies to deal with problems that previous generations of parents never had to cope with. Yet, at the same time, certain basic principles of good parenting never change. Let's start with "the basics" and then work toward the new, advanced skills that modern parents will need.*

For many generations the nature of parenting has remained the same: giving love and affection; providing for basic needs; inculcating a sense of pride, self-reliance, and judgment; and teaching the importance of education, of taking responsibility for one's own actions, and of having ethical standards. But few parents actually look forward to their child's adolescence with great enthusiasm. And few kids sail through adolescence without at least a few

---

* I am indebted to one of my former colleagues in the Adolescent Counseling Service, Dr. Alan Leiman, for his contribution to this discussion.

minor skirmishes with their parents. The breaking-away and letting-go processes virtually demand it. How you deal with these skirmishes can be crucial in determining the outcome of your teenager's adolescence. The key for parents of modern-day adolescents is to stay sane and survive with honor. There is simply no way to win a war with your children. But you have an important ally that you've never really considered—yourselves! Much of what will happen between the ages of twelve and twenty-one has been preordained by what has occurred during childhood. A child who has been taught to be self-reliant, independent, and confident and therefore carries a full tank of self-esteem into adolescence is unlikely to suffer any major disasters over the next decade of her life. The years between ages five and twelve are probably the most crucial in this regard. Now let's take a look at the most common areas of parent-teenager conflict and the strategies for dealing with them.

INDEPENDENCE VERSUS DEPENDENCE

The stereotypical teenager wants to be left alone, with no restrictions on his freedom and no responsibilities to weigh him down. Of course, he expects his laundry to be done just so, dinner on the table at the appointed hour, and the car always filled with gas. Parents may contribute to this conflict when they give their teenagers mixed messages: They expect their teenagers to be grown up enough to choose the right college, but don't trust them to shop for their own clothes.

Resolving the independence-versus-dependence conflict is a key task of adolescence and of parenting adolescents. Typically, teenagers irritate their parents by asking for—or demanding—all of the privileges of being an adult without being willing to accept any of the responsibilities.

Rather than criticizing their teenagers for being irresponsible, parents need to realize that it is their responsibility to teach their children *what responsibility entails.* Obviously, such lessons should begin long before adolescence. Young children and preteens should be given an allowance, do household chores, care for family pets, etc. But even in households where this has been the norm, parents frequently panic at the beginning of their children's adolescence. Many parents of twelve- or thirteen-year-olds feel that they can not possibly "immunize" their kids against all of the potential threats they will begin encountering. Consequently, they want to postpone the letting-go process—for the teenager's own good. But, as we've seen, sex education, drug education, and discussions about responsibility and morality all should have begun well before adolescence. When children turn into teenagers, parents often forget how important a role they have been playing in their lives. They have had over a decade to shape their child's thinking. Parents can use this influence to their advantage, as illustrated in the following two case studies, which typify the tug of war between independence and dependence.

□

Suzi: Suzi M. is a fifteen-year-old whose parents are extremely concerned about her choice of boyfriends. Although she is an honors student in tenth grade, her eighteen-year-old boyfriend, Doug, barely graduated from high school and now works part time as a mechanic. They are dating each other exclusively, and Mr. and Mrs. M. want Suzi to break off the relationship and see other (presumably more ambitious) boys. Mr. M. has now reached the point where he would like to forbid Suzi to see Doug altogether. Doug avoids coming to the M.

household. Mrs. M. is also concerned about Suzi's boy-friend but doesn't know how far to proceed with voicing her objections. She admits that Doug is always courteous with her, appears to treat Suzi well, is appropriately groomed, and seems intelligent. But she worries that things may "get serious," as Doug is not Suzi's intellectual match, nor will he be able to support her adequately.

❏

This is a situation that many parents dread, and it seems to occur more frequently with daughters than with sons. The question is, given that a relationship, of which you disapprove, is essentially a *fait accompli*, what should be your "strategy"? In this situation, if you forbid your daughter to see her boyfriend, she will find a way to see him surreptitiously. I have treated patients who would cut class in order to spend time with their boyfriends, or lied to their parents about their whereabouts and had friends cover for them. You would need the services of a full-time private detective to make sure that your prohibition was being observed. And even then, your daughter would never forgive you. Worse, if you had doubts about what your daughter and her boyfriend were up to sexually, she would gladly turn those doubts into a self-fulfilling prophecy and get pregnant. This was not a rare scenario in the Counseling Service, unfortunately. So what *are* your options?

In fact, you can use the amount of freedom that teen-agers have to your advantage. You do this by trusting them, explicitly and implicitly. After all, if your fifteen-year-old hasn't developed good judgment by her age, then something went wrong long before this boyfriend ever appeared. Consider what the following actually means to your teenager: "Sweetheart, you know we love you very much and want only the best for you. You're fifteen years old now, and we realize that, increasingly, you are going to be on your own. We'd be lying if we didn't tell you that we have some doubts about whether this is the right boy for you. But we also have to acknowledge that you are growing up and these are the kinds of decisions that you are going to have to make for yourself. He does seem to be a nice boy and apparently makes you happy. So we want you to know that we trust you and trust your judgment."

I know that this is incredibly difficult for parents to say —I've tried to teach it to many parents, and they tend to gag on some of the words. But consider the implications. First, your daughter now knows that you trust her. Second, you have been open and honest with her. Third, you have acknowledged the fact that she is becoming a young adult and therefore capable of making her own judgments. Fourth, you've eliminated the boyfriend as a factor in any kind of conflict or power struggle between you.

Now don't immediately expect your daughter to run right out and break up with him. But she may gradually lose interest if he represents her rebellion against you. On the other hand, she may have a genuine fondness for him, and you may be stuck with him for a while. Or you may be absolutely correct, and he turns out to be a disaster— but it takes your daughter a year or two to realize it. At age fifteen, it's important for your teenagers to start learning from their mistakes. And don't kid yourself—they *will* make mistakes. The trick is to support them, help them *learn* from their mistakes, and try to ensure that their mistakes are not life-threatening or lifelong. Of course, this reasoning does not hold if the boyfriend has recently been released on parole from state prison for cocaine possession and armed robbery!

In the M. family's situation, I would certainly make sure

that my daughter was being seen by a pediatrician or adolescent medicine specialist who could prescribe appropriate birth control for her, if necessary. The fact that
Suzi's boyfriend is three years older than she should serve
as an important clue to their evening activities. Suzi was
indeed sexually active with her boyfriend, and not using
any birth control. The most significant intervention we
made with the M. family was to make sure that Suzi had
a full gynecological evaluation and began using contraception. We could not persuade her parents to ignore Doug;
in fact, they first threatened him and then called his parents and tried to persuade them to end the relationship.
In return, Suzi threatened to run away. Yet, throughout
all of this conflict, she remained an honors student. Had
she become pregnant, Suzi might have felt compelled to
marry Doug, or to have an abortion, or she might have
chosen to carry the pregnancy to term. None of the different scenarios would have provided a very satisfactory outcome, so I feel we made significant progress with the M.
family, even though we could not do as much as we
would have liked to end the parent-teenager turmoil.

❑

*JEREMY: Jeremy is a fourteen-year-old who was sent from
school for an evaluation of his behavior. During the past
six months he has become increasingly disruptive in class,
although his grades have remained mostly B's and C's.
His teachers report that he seems unhappy. When I interview Jeremy with his parents, I ask them to describe an
average day: Jeremy storms downstairs every morning,
demanding his breakfast. His mother angrily sends him
back upstairs to make his bed and clean up his room. In
the evening, his parents repeatedly have to insist that he
turn down the stereo. He denies that it's too loud and tells*

*them to go to bed. When I ask about enjoyable family
activities, the parents and son look at each other in complete surprise, realizing that they never even have dinners
together, much less take vacations or outings.*

❑

In such a stressed family, the development of an independent, well-adjusted adolescent would seem impossible. Clearly, a teenager's bid for independence will result
in some stress to the family, since parental values are
often being rejected, or at least questioned. How can such
stress be minimized? Four factors are crucial in raising
independent, mature young adults rather than immature
adolescent rebels: communicating effectively, enhancing a
teenager's self-image, teaching effective decision making,
and disciplining effectively. Each is worth examining in
some detail.

Family Communication

The family therapy movement has revolutionized thinking about how families communicate. Families can be defined as being functional or dysfunctional depending on
the **clarity, completeness,** and **congruence** of the communication among their members.

Clarity is illustrated by the following example: You tell
your teenage daughter to be home before dark every day,
but she invariably comes in an hour late. An argument
develops each night. You angrily point outside and show
her that it is already dark. She insists that it was still light
when she left her friend's house and that in fact, it's still
not really dark outside. This conflict easily could have
been avoided if your instructions had consisted of "Please
be home by six o'clock."

Completeness involves the explicitness of instructions. The father who criticizes his son for not trimming the hedges after mowing the lawn—not because he had specifically asked his son to, but because the youngster "should have known to do it anyway"—is exhibiting incomplete communication. Teenagers are too self-absorbed to be very effective mind readers.

Congruence means the extent to which verbal communication (words) and nonverbal communications (gestures, voice inflections, body language) match. When they do, communication is enhanced. When they don't, people get very confused, and in families serious pathology can result. For example, if you ask someone how he is feeling and he answers, "Fine," but then groans and holds his head in his hands, his response is incongruent. Incongruence is sometimes also referred to as giving "double messages." A mother who had a repressive upbringing and who wants to talk with her daughter about the miracle of love and sex might betray herself because of the tension in her voice or her signs of embarrassment. She would do far better to acknowledge her discomfort about the subject, preface her talk with a description of how her own parents tried to deal with it, and admit that she does not want her daughter to have the same anxieties about sex that she had.

Good communication does not stop with the ability to talk effectively with your child, however. Just as important is the ability to be a good listener. We all know people who are either good or bad listeners. What makes them one way or the other? The ability to acknowledge feelings and reflect them is crucial: "I can see why you feel that way." "You seem down today." "I'd be bothered by that too. Is there anything you can do about it?" Strong feelings tend to diminish in intensity when there is a sympathetic listener on the other end. Parents can accomplish a great deal of valuable emotional first aid. Equally as important in dealing with teenagers is never to deny their perceptions. Your daughter comes home and is upset because she didn't make the cheerleading squad. You immediately smile, because it reminds you of some triumph or failure of your own when you were her age and because you know how transient a setback this is. But to your daughter it could mean that the end of the world is at hand. I've treated teenagers who attempted suicide because they didn't make the cheerleading squad. You don't have to share her perceptions—and in all likelihood you won't, because you have a mature, adult view of the world and therefore can keep things in perspective. But you must be able to *sympathize* with her perceptions and treat them as important. They *are* important, especially because she has chosen to share them with you.

Enhancing a Teenager's Self-image

Good listening also falls into the category of enhancing a teenager's self-image. You know this from your everyday experience: There are people who listen to you and are looking at the traffic out the window; there are those who nod and you know that they're thinking about what they're going to have for dinner; and then there are your friends, who actively listen, reflect your feelings, and make you feel good about yourself. Educators seem enamored of the idea that self-esteem is like a vaccine that can be administered in a few discrete doses. It's not: Self-esteem is more like a sand dune that can be slowly built up or eroded, depending on the tide.

Early in their child's development, parents need to begin to identify those areas in which the child is unique or talented. If your child is not a terrific student or athlete, this may take some creativity on your part. It may be your child's interest in animals, or his exceptional friendliness, or his unselfishness. Every child has some area in which he is unique or talented, and it is important that every parent discover what that area is—the sooner the better. On a larger scale, an example of this kind of creativity is the Special Olympics, which gives developmentally delayed or handicapped youth an opportunity for recognition and success.

Acknowledging the inevitable—that your kids are growing up—is another way to help their self-esteem begin to accrue. It is a standard joke that one reason grandparents and grandchildren get along so well is that they share a common enemy. But, in fact, grandparents tend to take young people's impending adulthood as a fact of life, and teenagers respond well to that kind of acceptance and trust. Some experts even believe that the sooner you can take your teenager's adulthood for granted, the sooner she will assume that role. This all sounds fine, but how exactly do you accomplish it? One way is to avoid the standard parental admonishments: "I'm surprised at you," "I know you could have done better." How would *you* like it if you invited me to your home for dinner and spent all day preparing a fine meal, and at the end of it I sat back and said, "That was great. But I know you could have done better"? Another parental favorite to avoid at all costs is the phrase "when I was your age." It tends to cause instant deafness in teenagers. Many of us would like to be able to give to our children the gift of our experience, as if it were a Christmas present. Unfortunately, we can't. Experience is personal and idiosyncratic and, almost by definition, is not transferable.

Enhancing and preserving self-esteem is also accomplished by learning how to criticize your teenager or be angry with him. When things are going wrong for him is not the right time to begin informing your teenager about the flaws you've detected in his personality. Criticizing teenagers is like doing surgery: It always hurts, and it is sometimes fatal.

Please don't misunderstand me: I'm not trying to tell you that you should never get angry or upset with your teenager. We're talking about *style* here. After all, fifty million American parents can't be wrong: Teenagers are perfectly capable of dumb or immature behavior. But, as you are getting angry, remember to deal with the situation at hand and not attack his personality or character. In other words, "anger without insult," as Haim Ginott wrote in his famous book, *Between Parent & Teenager*. To borrow one of his examples: Your teenage son takes a shower before a big date and makes a complete mess of the bathroom—wet towels strewn everywhere, hair in the tub, shaving cream in the sink, etc. You are entitled to be angry. But consider the impact of two different things you could say to him: (A) "Barry, you slob. No girl is ever going to want you for a husband. She'll be picking up after you for the rest of her life. Whoever taught you to be such a one-man wrecking crew? Certainly not your father or me." (B) "Barry, it makes me very angry to see the bathroom left in such a condition. Would you mind cleaning it up a bit before you leave for your date?" Remember that self-esteem is precious and transient, and it can be slowly eroded without much effort. The first response may help *you* feel better, but it has the potential to devastate your teenager. He may, in fact, be thinking very similar things about his date: How can she like someone like me? Why does she find me attractive? The second response treats him as a responsible citizen who has made a mistake but has the power to rectify it.

The flip side of learning how to be angry is learning how to praise teenagers. It can be equally as treacherous. Why? Because praise represents an evaluation and is being done by someone who is sitting in judgment. Teenagers have nearly as much difficulty dealing with praise as with criticism. Therefore, any attempts to praise your teenager should follow the same guidelines: Praise should describe efforts and accomplishments, not evaluate personality or character traits.

However, 1990s parents please take note: "Self-esteem" has become the buzz word of our era. It is probably not the cure-all that many educators and health professionals think it is. Many people talk about self-esteem as if it were contained in a vial and given in doses like a drug. In fact, self-esteem begins to form long before adolescence—probably in utero, as reflected in parents' self-perceptions and their attitudes about themselves, their future, and their baby. If you're worrying about your teenager's self-esteem, you might find comfort in knowing that great thinkers like Freud asserted that the ego is most completely shaped in the first year of life. Erikson agreed, but emphasized that the development of one's self-image accelerates during adolescence and represents the most crucial developmental task during those years. While many educators talk about anti-this and anti-that programs at school, designed to increase self-esteem in their students, in fact self-esteem stays very close to home. The early childhood years are probably the most important in inculcating a sense of security, trust, and love. But the middle childhood and preteen years are probably when self-esteem can be most actively enhanced by parents. These years are crucial ones for finding a positive niche for your child.

Decision Making

This task is a particularly difficult one because parents have to balance the dual goals of allowing adolescents to begin making their own decisions (and their own mistakes) with structure, limits, and occasionally no choice in certain matters. Priorities are key. Parents need to decide what is and is not negotiable. If something is nonnegotiable, it should be clearly stated as a house rule—for example, no television viewing until all homework is completed. These are the rules that the teenager must obey, like it or not, and for which "Because I'm the dad" may be an entirely appropriate explanation. If the number of such rules is not large and they do not differ grossly from other parents' rules in the community, reluctant compliance can be expected.

The negotiable areas allow teenagers to learn decision-making skills. At times the national anthem of adolescence seems to be "Don't Fence Me In." With negotiable areas, parents can offer the teenager a set of alternatives from which to choose. It is a simple fact of human nature that people respond better to options than to orders. If your boss says, "Do this report by Tuesday," you may bristle. Or she can say, "I need this report done by next Tuesday. Do you think you can do it? Should I give it to Jones instead? I can offer you some extra help, or take one of the other projects off your desk for a while." Although the task may seem insurmountable, you are being given several choices. By showing some respect for you as an individual, capable of making choices, your boss encourages your cooperation.

Setting appropriate limits—establishing the borders of the "corral"—is one of the most difficult aspects of parenting. The bigger the corral, the more freedom the teenager senses, even though you have set the crucial boundaries. For example, your teenager wants to go to the junior prom. A group of his friends are getting together afterward and renting a hotel room and want him to pitch in. He wants to hire a limo to impress his date. Of course, there's also the cost of the tickets, his tuxedo, and a corsage. You can't afford this total package, nor are you at all comfortable with the hotel room idea. You can "just say no" to any or all of it, but that isn't going to score you a lot of points in any popularity contest. Nor is this one of those issues that call for parental tyranny. The corral becomes whatever amount you feel you can afford. If you agree to give him seventy-five dollars, suggest that he can do whatever he wants with the money. If he'd rather spend money on a limo rental than a corsage, that's up to him. Also, part of the corral is his curfew—say, 3 A.M. If he wants to stop by at his friends' hotel room, that's up to him, but he must be home by 3 A.M. If he wants to use some of the money to help his buddies pay for the hotel room, that's fine too, although both you and he know this would not be the best use of his limited funds. Of course, the usual prohibitions against drinking and other drugs are not at issue here, because those are house rules. You and I might think that a teenager riding in a limo is not only silly but extravagant. But if it's really that important to him, then this is one of those issues that is not worth contesting.

Issues on which parents and teenagers frequently disagree, such as chores, curfews, and allowance, are very amenable to negotiation and compromise and don't require major confrontations. Again, a corral approach can be effective here as well. Let's say that you are trying to get your daughter to do the dishes. "Would you like to do the dishes now? If so, I can help you. But you can do them anytime before bed if you'd like." No one likes to be told, "Do this, now. Period. No discussion." It's demeaning. Parents sometimes exclude their children from certain decisions, assuming that they and the teenager are irreconcilably apart. Deciding on a curfew, for example, may involve a difference of only an hour or so, or an exception can made for a special occasion. The parents may assume that the teenager will settle for nothing earlier than 5 A.M. (and the teen may assume that the parents want him safely tucked into his bed by 10 P.M.). For negotiable items that require a yes-or-no response rather than a series of choices, parents need to communicate that "we value your input." Although the final decision may be the parents' in these situations, the teenager's opinion is still given serious consideration.

Given the fact that teenagers are not adults, parents must also expect that some of the teen's decisions will not be good ones. In fact, some of their decisions may be completely self-serving, immature, or even dangerous. But, within reason, teenagers have to learn to cope with their own mistakes. So when your teenage daughter comes to you to ask how to get out of a date because another boy just phoned her and she said yes to him, too, it is crucial that she learn how to deal with such matters, albeit with your guidance, if you so choose. After all, if she can't make this sort of easy decision and face up to the consequences, what is she going to do when she has to decide about far more crucial things, like when to begin having sexual intercourse, whether to smoke, and when to begin drinking?

Some teenagers are more reserved and have difficulty making decisions or involving themselves in constructive outside activities that might serve to promote self-esteem and develop peer relationships. With these kids, the "choice within choices" technique can also be useful—for example, "We think it would be a good idea for you to get involved in some activity. It can be athletics, a church group, scouting, whatever [within the limits of cost and ability to transport the child]. We would like you to try it for a trial period of two months. If after that time you decide that you don't like it, we'll consider something else." In many cases teenagers will choose something, reluctantly at first, and gradually become more absorbed in the activity.

Discipline

Discipline is one area in which many of our parents were extremely old-fashioned. Consequently, we may find ourselves either overreacting in the opposite direction—being too lenient—or using their system because it's the only one we're familiar with.

Discipline is a frequently misunderstood concept and one that can easily be abused. Parents seem bent on equating discipline with punishment, even though most psychologists would agree that positive reinforcement, not negative reinforcement, is a far more powerful tool for behavior modification. Parents mostly reject the classic behavior modification techniques for fear of having to "bribe" their children. Since you probably were raised by parents who used more negative than positive reinforcement, I won't try to persuade you how important the latter is or how effective it can be. But I will say that all punishments are not created equal and that there is an art in knowing how and when to punish.

Punishment has been defined as the infliction of an unpleasant experience in order to modify future behavior. Therefore, the goal is not to hurt the child, but rather to minimize the chance of the undesirable behavior's recurring. Punishment is effective when the child has some sense that he has done wrong, he has some respect for the punisher, and the punishment fits the crime. For example, Sonny gets an F on a homework assignment that he failed to do, so his parents decide to forbid him to go to a party that weekend. This inflicts an unpleasant experience on him, but it has no logical connection to the undesirable behavior. On the other hand, a new house rule that homework must be completed before watching television, going to hang out with friends, or using the telephone—especially if these are the reasons the homework wasn't completed—may not be appreciated by the youngster but at least is likely to make sense to him. In the Counseling Service we often evaluated teenagers who were star athletes. For some relatively trivial offense like "talking back," their parents would threaten them with not being allowed to compete in an upcoming event. Knowing where your child is vulnerable does not mean that you can attack indiscriminately. Indeed, such maneuvers can be counterproductive: His athletic prowess may be the only thing helping to boost his self-confidence and self-esteem. Prohibiting him from playing a sport or competing in a meet may serve only to increase his resentment of you, without teaching him any lessons about whatever behavior was objectionable in the first place.

There are several important principles of punishment:

Parents should never punish in anger. The parents who sit up until 2 A.M., waiting for their curfew-breaking daughter, might be wiser to say, "We'll talk about your punishment in the morning."

Punishment should be done privately. The parents who embarrass their daughter in front of her date will have a very difficult time getting her to comply with *anything* the next morning.

Effective punishment should be meted out as quickly as possible after the offense. This helps to associate the punishment with the crime; families with pets can understand that a lapse in a pet's bowel control cannot be effectively punished an hour after the accident occurs. It also eliminates the "wait until your father comes home" fallacy.

The punishment should be only severe enough to elimi-nate the probability that the undesirable behavior will recur. Grounding a teenager for six weeks for coming home an hour past curfew is excessive, and counterpro-ductive to a healthy parent-child relationship.

Parents must present a united front when a punishment has been decided upon.

Punishment must be consistently applied. One would be wiser to make no threats at all than to make threats that cannot or will not be carried out.

Only the youngster should be punished, not the rest of the family.

The punishment should target the offense, not its perpe-trator. Punishments that attack the teen's self-esteem are likely to become self-fulfilling prophecies.

Perhaps the most important single principle in disci-pline is "Tolerate much, but sanction little." A privilege should not be rescinded automatically because it is abused the first time it's used; mistakes and pushing the bound-aries have to be expected from teenagers. The best exam-ple of the difference between sanctioning and tolerating is the sort of patient I am beginning to see in increasing numbers: the fifteen-year-old girl who has told her mother that she is having sex, and whose mother brings her to see me for a pelvic exam and appropriate contraception. Does the mother sanction the girl's sexual activity? No. But, given the possible repercussions, she is willing to tolerate it and even see that her daughter receives the proper medical care rather than, for instance, kicking her out of the house. In such situations, the mother often continues to make it clear to the teenager that she does not approve of the sexual activity. However, she also ac-knowledges that she has little direct control or choice in the matter. With the spectrum of authority ranging from a laissez-faire attitude to a militaristic absolutism, parents need to understand that finding the midpoint is crucial. Both extremes are likely to lead to teenagers with behavior disturbances. On the other hand, a midpoint that leaves the final decision up to the adults but allows the teenager ample room to try things out and make her own mistakes will result in a healthier and happier teen.

PARENTING RESILIENT CHILDREN

> *"The world breaks everyone, and afterwards many are strong in the broken places."*
>
> —ERNEST HEMINGWAY,
> *A Farewell to Arms*

> *"Success is nothing more than going from failure to failure with enthusiasm."*
>
> —WINSTON CHURCHILL

Mahskroosbarn is Swedish for "dandelion child": a child who can grow and thrive anywhere. Given the complexities of modern civilization, especially American society, we need to examine how we can raise our children to be "unbreakable."

Dr. Thomas Boyce, a pediatrician and researcher at the University of San Francisco School of Medicine, has spent much of his career examining childhood stress and why certain kids seem immune to it while others are particularly vulnerable. He and a number of other talented researchers have done studies around the world to identify the characteristics of "the unbreakable child": the child who thrives in the midst of poverty or civil unrest. If we can understand how children survive the worst-case situations, perhaps it will give us clues to raising them in our society, where the stresses are not so extreme. The four main characteristics of children in these studies who were successful in overcoming the stresses of their environment were: They had easy, responsive temperaments; they came from close and coherent families; they had social support from friends and relatives; and they had an individual sense of purpose and destiny.

According to Dr. Boyce, this all adds up to the child's ability to answer four important questions: "Who am I?" "Am I loved?" "Whom can I count on?" "What am I here for?" Raise your children so that they can answer these questions and you'll have happy, successful, *resilient* children, able to survive "the slings and arrows of outrageous Fortune." Granted, your child's temperament may have a genetic component that you can do nothing about. But the other components of "the unbreakable child" are achievable. How?

Encourage self-reliance, a sense of mastery, and controlled *risk taking in your children.* Adolescence is too late to begin doing this—childhood and preadolescence are far preferable. Think about how you treated your teenager as a baby. When she rolled over successfully, did you give her a round of applause? Did you encourage her to crawl to her favorite toy, rather than handing it to her? Sound trivial? Perhaps, but self-esteem is built in slow, trivial steps, not infused in one massive dose. Modern parents sometimes look for the quick fix, waving flash cards in their kid's face when he is fifteen months old. The idea that parents can create "superchildren" is a myth, helped along by a toy and baby product industry that stands to profit from it. Children learn at their own speed and in their own time. There is no evidence, for example, that the child who can read at age three has any long-term advantage over other children.

Accomplishing this task may require pushing your pre-teenager to try unknown things—perhaps overnight camp, swimming, or acting. The expression on children's faces when they discover that they can do something that they had previously thought was impossible is really priceless.

Encouraging self-reliance also involves close attention to those self-esteem–sparing principles outlined above. And there may be some significant differences between boys and girls. Some new research by Dr. Carol Gilligan, a professor of education at Harvard, has found that a majority of nine-year-old girls are confident and assertive and feel good about themselves, but less than a third feel the same way at age fifteen. Boys' self-esteem also declined with age, but to a lesser degree. Obviously, there are many questions about how to raise children and teenagers that remain unanswered and will require further research.

A sense of mastery comes with supervised play, exposure to a variety of activities, and opportunities to learn more about the world. That goes directly against the concept of "quality time," because it involves quantity of time as well as quality. It means offering children an educational alternative to the three to four hours a day they currently spend parked in front of the TV. Given the current American Academy of Pediatrics' recommendation of no more than one to two hours of TV a day, that leaves one to three hours that must be filled. Reading to your children, telling stories, going on nature walks, investigating the zoo or a museum, camping, bicycling—all are far more educational, creative, and interactive than television, but all require more time and parental commitment. If both parents work, this may require scheduling so that each is free during some part of the weekend day to relax or get work done.

A sense of mastery also comes when parents are able to discover the unique qualities and talents of their children. This may require some experimentation—dance lessons, music lessons, horseback riding lessons, etc.—and some parents may not be able to afford to have their kids sample such a variety of activities. But children do not need expensive toys to enjoy themselves thoroughly. And this is one of the most crucial tasks that parents must accomplish if they want to produce happy and successful future adults.

Allowing children and teenagers to take *controlled risks* is a new concept for the 1990s. It derives from research that demonstrates that many adolescents have an innate need for risk-taking activities, which can involve seeing what their new bodies are capable of (sex or drugs) or seeing how much they can get away with (driving after drinking, or taking an exam without having studied for it). The idea is to fulfill this need with safe and controlled activities rather than unsafe and unsupervised ones. Children are born risk takers: Many toddlers love to jump off furniture, whether you're there to catch them or not. Many older children love roller-coaster rides, much to the dismay of their motion-sick parents. There is something intrinsically thrilling about speed, motion, jumping off high places without a safety net and living to tell about it (hence bungee jumping).

Although there is little current research about whether this concept will definitely succeed in producing healthier teenagers, it does have a certain commonsense rationality to it. And there *are* good data to suggest that teenagers heavily involved in organized sports are far less likely to use drugs on a regular basis (the one exception being anabolic steroids). Programs such as Outward Bound can be extremely useful to parents and their teenagers. So, too, can such more mundane activities as allowing them to take the bus by themselves to meet a friend, go to the mall by themselves, or stay at home without a baby sitter. Certain adult sports also have an appeal for certain teenagers

—mountain biking, rock climbing, scuba diving, hang gliding. All are examples of risk-taking behaviors that adults engage in but rarely question.

Allowing your preteens and teens to take risks may involve allowing them to do something "impractical," like taking Italian instead of Spanish in school, or taking acting classes one summer instead of going to computer camp. Or it might mean something considerably more dangerous—allowing them to go rock climbing or canoeing and camping in the wilderness with an explorer group. Not all kids are eager risk takers, and many will be happy simply to continue along in their normal everyday activities. But those who are more adventurous will welcome these sorts of challenges. And there is no question that organized thrill seeking is far preferable to the more random risk taking of sex, drugs, and reckless driving during adolescence.

Develop strong, predictable family routines and rituals. We do this automatically when our children are babies: Our primary goal is to "get them on a schedule." But somehow we forget how much children thrive on schedules, predictability, routines, and rituals. Divorce can threaten predictability, but parents who are sensitive to this issue and are able to maintain their children's routines as much as possible will be surprised at how unaffected their children may be by the divorce. In many American families dinnertime always served the purpose of bringing the family together, but this ritual has now lost out to Nintendo and two-career families. Some of our fondest memories of childhood are often about vacationing at the same spot year after year, whether it's camping in the mountains or staying at a tacky motel near the seashore. Birthdays represent one of childhood's greatest rituals, as does Thanksgiving.

Provide and offer social support. All parents need to strive to become open and approachable. Parenting books can sometimes help here, as can discussions with friends who seem to have a knack with their own kids. Extended families can be extremely helpful here as well. Parents should rejoice if their teenager feels especially close to an uncle, or even a friend's parent, rather than feeling jealous about another adult's relationship with their child. Teachers are also extremely important in this regard and can serve as surrogate parents in the right situations. But parents must remember that their primary role is that of parent, not best friend.

The Importance of the Family Unit

Child psychologists in the sixties and seventies who supported the notion of a "democratic family" were misunderstood. Successful parents more closely resemble benevolent monarchs than presidents of a democracy. Giving children and teenagers choices is an excellent idea —when it is appropriate. As discussed, some things are negotiable (curfew, allowance); other things are not (drugs). Young people need a firm hand, but not an arbitrary or unyielding one.

Increasingly during the past decade, psychologists have acknowledged that the family unit should come first, and children afterward. This means that the normal self-centeredness of children must be modified somehow, since all babies develop, by necessity, a feeling that Mom and Dad are there to satisfy their needs. Inevitably, going from self-centeredness to family-centeredness will cause some turmoil. This is the origin of the "terrible twos," the age at which the child's drive for autonomy begins to emerge. For some unknown reason, parents have latched on to the foolish notion that a child's self-esteem comes from the amount of attention she gets. This is a particularly destructive concept when applied to a two-year-old, who will eagerly soak up any attention and bank it away as self-centeredness. The important lesson for parents to learn is that attention does not equal love or self-esteem. So how do you accomplish the transition from the child's Copernican view of the world to a more Galilean concept? According to psychologist John Rosemond (*Albuquerque Journal*, April 24, 1991):

> By making time for the marriage on a regular basis. By not catering to the child's whims, whether emotional or material. By expecting obedience, and enforcing it firmly, but gently. By presenting a united front. By acting like you know what you are doing.

At times this may be difficult for you, no question about it. We want to make our kids happy, and we seem to have at hand many of the material resources to do so. But happy in the short run is miserable in the long run, because you are liable to create a child who believes that you exist simply to please him. Based on my work with adolescents, it does not seem too farfetched to me to suggest that an overly indulged "terrible two" might result in a troubled adolescent.

Let me give you a specific example: Your sixteen-year-old son has maintained a 3.5 average and will graduate from high school in a year. He is planning on going to college and talks about continuing on to business school. Although you and he have had your quarrels, he is turning out to be a delightful young man, and you couldn't be more pleased. You and your spouse are both working and have saved two thousand dollars in a rainy-day account. You both feel that you could really use a vacation, just the two of you, but perhaps you have read a book like this one that tells you how important positive reinforcement is. So instead you decide to pay your son's way to Europe (where you haven't been for ten years) so he can travel with his best friend for the summer. Thoughtful idea? Yes. Good idea? Not really. First, your marriage comes first. If you want to spend the money, go to Europe yourselves. Take your son with you if you want to. (If he wants to go to Europe with his friend, offer to finance 50 percent of the trip, but not the entire amount. Alternatively, put the money into a savings bond or certificate of deposit for him, to be used for business school expenses.) A smaller, less expensive token of your affection makes far more sense, given the primacy of your marriage.

The Importance of Educating Your Child

You can no longer leave sex education, drug education, and education about your basic values to the schools or churches, or simply sit back and hope for the best. Teaching your children about these issues is your responsibility as a parent, and if you shirk this responsibility, either your child's peers or the TV set will take over. Given the power of an adolescent's peer group and the current state of the American media, that's not something I would recommend.

In the 1990s, educating your child means facing up to some very unpleasant realities—sexual abuse, for one. Many surveys have found that as many as one in four adult women report having been sexually abused as children or teenagers. You must teach your children how they can protect themselves and that no one has the right to touch their bodies without their consent. This becomes particularly important as they start dating.

Being a parent in the 1990s also means that you will need to play more of a censorship role than perhaps you would like or would feel comfortable with, particularly if you are fairly liberal. As children of the sixties, we may remember how old-fashioned our parents' generation seemed and therefore tend to be too permissive about such issues. But remember that censorship has always fallen within the purview of parenting; children have no First Amendment rights. In fact, sometimes they require protection when we adults feel compelled to exercise our own. If this means that you will be labeled "old-fashioned" by your kids, so be it. Our parents were right about this, and they didn't even have to face the onslaught of the modern media. Once you acknowledge the importance and potential influence of the media in their lives, you've *got* to shield them from the harmful excesses. As we've discussed, this means limiting their TV time, watching TV and movies with them, and monitoring what TV shows and movies are appropriate for them to watch. If you think about it, this sort of scrutiny is really nothing new—most parents already carefully monitor what their children are reading. It simply extends your influence to the wider range of media that have emerged since we were children.

The Importance of Parents' Peer Groups

Not only are modern parents "media-savvy," they understand and appreciate normal adolescent psychology, especially the role of the peer group. Although the peer group's influence lessens as teenagers reach middle and late adolescence, it never fades away completely. We are all influenced by our age-related peers, but this is not necessarily harmful. Just as parents of babies often compare notes about their infants' development, parents of teenagers need to compare notes—and to try to agree on common rules about such activities as supervision and drinking at teenagers' parties. The divide-and-conquer

strategy that is an integral part of every child's armamen-
tarium doesn't work against a united front. Discussion
groups at your church, synagogue, or school could be
extremely useful to you. Parents do not necessarily have
to agree on such issues as curfews and privileges, but
one set of parents who thinks it is fine to buy a keg for a
sixteenth-birthday party, or to go out of town and leave
their teenager alone in the house, is all that it takes to
undermine your most vigilant efforts.

SINGLE PARENTING

Almost by definition, modern parenting *is* single parenting for more than fifteen million American children and
adolescents, according to 1988 figures. Nearly one-quarter
of all children in the United States grow up with only one
parent. Divorce and separation account for the majority of
one-parent households. In chapter 2 we discussed some
general principles surrounding divorce and its impact on
young people in the short term. Now let's examine some
of the more long-term issues involved in single parenting
(see appendix I for a list of books that deal with this important issue in more detail).

Parents who have lost a spouse to divorce or death
share a number of similarities with their teenagers: the
need to redefine their identities, to explore their newfound independence, to establish sexual relationships,
and to identify a means of support. Parents who find
themselves struggling with these objectives may feel that
they have precious little time to help their teenagers cope
with them as well. Having the primary or sole responsibility for the children may feel like an undue burden, yet
there can be a positive side to this as well. Decisions are
much simpler when only one person has to be the decision maker, particularly when the parents frequently dis-

agreed about discipline or basic values. Parent-child communication can also be more direct. As the parent and child struggle simultaneously to solve similar problems, the child may even develop a degree of empathy for the parent.

Invariably, sex becomes the number one issue between single parents and their children. Teenagers from single-parent families are more likely to begin having sexual intercourse at a young age than teens from intact families. As the single parent begins to date, she may become confused about the amount of freedom people have today compared to when she dated as a teenager or young adult. At the same time, she still feels the need to serve as a good role model for her children and knows that her teenagers will pounce on any real or imagined act of hypocrisy, such as allowing a date to sleep over but forbidding a teenager's date to do the same. This scenario does not have one "right" solution because the outcome depends largely on the parent's ethical standards. But it does call for some rather frank discussion between parent and child. And it does have a "wrong" solution: allowing the teenager the same rights and privileges as the parent. Despite their inevitable protests, teenagers want guidance from their parents, *not* equality, and will actually be reassured when they receive the former rather than the latter.

Probably the most difficult aspect of single parenting from the parent's viewpoint is financial. With one income gone, the family's financial status will inevitably decline, often even if alimony and child support are paid. And since alimony is being awarded less frequently, and child support is rarely enforced, many women find themselves in a very precarious situation financially. Frequently that translates into having to move into a new house or apartment, having less money for clothes and entertainment, and taking no vacations. For the mother, it may mean having to return to the job market for the first time in many years, or accept a menial second job solely for the income. High school dropout rates are higher for teenagers from single-parent families. Such teens may resent the new economic restrictions and may try to break away early to seek their own fortune. Here, again, communication between parent and teenager will be at a premium and may help to allay some of the teen's anxieties or feelings.

If parenting in the 1990s is as stressful as I've sometimes made it seem, at least you can derive some comfort in knowing that, increasingly, help is available. Adolescent medicine has become a new medical subspecialty. Thousands of young pediatricians and family practitioners are being trained in how to care for teenagers, and help you care for your teenagers. And organizations like the American Academy of Pediatrics, the Society for Adolescent Medicine, the American College of Obstetricians and Gynecologists, and even the American Medical Association are getting involved. In the next chapter we will discuss how teenagers are being treated differently by the medical establishment than when we were growing up, how you can use your pediatrician or family physician as a "surrogate parent," and when your teenager may need the services of a psychologist or psychiatrist.

Chapter 7

Difficult Teenagers and New Support Systems

❑

I would like to love you but you're not very lovable.

—THORNTON WILDER,
The Skin of Our Teeth

Are you lost daddy I asked tenderly.
Shut up he explained.

—RING LARDNER,
"The Young Immigrunts"

❑

MONICA: *Monica is a vivacious fourteen-year-old who has always been extremely popular at school. She is an A student and likes to run cross-country. To keep her weight down, she has been dieting for the past six months. Her favorite hobby seems to be helping her mother cook, although she rarely eats much. Lately she has seemed thinner and more fatigued than usual, and her parents have heard her vomiting once or twice. For several months she has been allowed to date "in groups," although she doesn't seem eager to do so. Her mother doesn't think that she could possibly be pregnant, but asks anyway. Monica's response is "Mother, please. Get a life." When I saw her, Monica was five feet six inches and weighed 96 pounds (down from her normal weight of 120 pounds). Her parents are worried that she has an ulcer.*

BENNY: *Benny is a sixteen-year-old who has never "performed up to his potential," according to his parents. Although his IQ is high, he struggles to make C's and D's. He appears uninterested in school and has no career plans. For the past six months he has been keeping odd hours. Attempts to establish a curfew or to ground him have been ignored—he walks out of the house. Since Benny is bigger than his parents, they have been unable to stop him. They have both smelled marijuana smoke in his room, but he denies that he is using it and tells them to stop being "paranoid." He obtained a driver's license when he turned sixteen, five months ago, and recently was cited for speeding. Two months ago he was suspended from school for a week for breaking two windows in the gym.*

❑

Most parents would agree that both Monica and Benny are in big trouble, and they would be correct. Monica has an eating disorder—anorexia nervosa—and Benny has a psychiatric disorder and a learning disability and is heavily involved in using drugs. Surprisingly, both sets of parents denied for several months that their teenager had a serious illness. What should they have done?

They should have taken their teenagers to see their pediatrician or family physician. Increasingly, physicians are being taught about the complexities of adolescent medicine. Most licensing boards now insist that interns and residents have at least some significant training in this area, so your "baby doctor" may be fully capable of treating teenagers and young adults as well. Your family physician may also feel at ease with teenagers and often is able to cope with the gynecological aspects of adolescent health care. Some of my colleagues may not appreciate this, but the physicians to avoid—*unless they have a specific interest in and affinity for adolescents*—are internists, gynecologists, and subspecialists (such as an allergist or cardiologist), unless you have been referred by your primary-care physician. The reason I am being so hard on internists and gynecologists is that they are trained specifically to see adult patients, not adolescents. Although not all adolescents need to be seen by an adolescent medicine specialist, your doctor must have an *interest* in and *expertise* in treating adolescent patients or he may do more harm than good. Adolescents are neither children nor adults. If your physician makes the mistake of treating them as one or the other, his rapport with them will be nil. Adolescents also have their own unique diseases (such as acne) and their own unique way of reacting to them. I have seen teenagers taken to surgery unnecessarily, subjected to numerous unnecessary tests, or given erroneous diagnoses, all because the doctor didn't understand the basic principles of adolescent medicine.

How can you know if primary-care physicians are comfortable with teenagers? First, you can ask them. Next, if they are Board-certified in either Pediatrics or Family Medicine, there is a good chance that they are. Third, you can ask the Society for Adolescent Medicine for the name of an adolescent medicine specialist in your area, and phone her to ask for a recommendation. Fourth, you will be able to tell after your teenager's first visit to the doctor. If, during a routine comprehensive exam, the doctor fails to ask teenagers about their schoolwork, whether they are sexually active, whether they are smoking or drinking or using other drugs, then the doctor is not doing a proper job. This is how your physician can serve as a "parent surrogate," and it's important for you to understand how your relationship with your pediatrician, for instance, will have to change from when your teenager was a baby.

❑

TONY: Tony is a sixteen-year-old who comes to see me because it hurts when he urinates. This has been occurring for several days. When I ask Tony if he is sexually active, he rolls his eyes. I explain that I am asking only in order to be able to care for his problem and that whatever he tells me will remain confidential. He asks me which girlfriend I think gave this to him. After a physical exam and a few simple laboratory tests, I determine that Tony has gonorrhea. I treat him with the appropriate antibiotics and reassure him that he will improve. I also tell him that I will have to make a report to the state department of health, and they will want to contact him about his partners; or he should feel free to have them call me and come in for treatment. He promises he will do this.

Several days later I receive a phone call from Tony's mother. Why was Tony seeing me? Is there anything wrong? I explain to her that Tony is now old enough to receive what we call confidential health care. In other words, I am Tony's doctor, not his mother's doctor, and therefore I need Tony's permission to divulge any information. She says she understands completely, but Tony said it would be okay to tell her everything. I say that's very nice, I'll be happy to confirm it with Tony when I see him in a few days for a re-check, and I'll call her then.

When Tony comes back a few days later, I tell him about the phone call. "By the way, did you want me to tell your mother about your visit?" I ask. His eyes become as big as Frisbees. "Hell, no!"

❑

Those of us who specialize in adolescent medicine sometimes get a bad rep. People think that we are antiparent, or that we are deliberately trying to conceal important information from parents. Nothing could be further from the truth, so far as I'm concerned. Parents are crucial to adolescents, in a whole host of ways—far more important than adolescent medicine specialists! But there are times when—how can I say this diplomatically?—parents get in the way (though often it's not even their fault). For example: treating teenagers who think that they may have a sexually transmitted disease. If teenagers think that the physician will pick up the phone and call their parents and tell them that they've been having sex and now they've got an STD, they'll never come in to get treated in the first place. And then we've got an even bigger public health problem. For this reason, every state in the country has a law that specifically allows teenagers to be seen for confidential health care if they suspect that they might have an STD. Many states add: or if they suspect they could be pregnant. And most states also mandate confidential diagnosis and treatment for drug abuse as well. Are states antiparent? No. This is an example of how two interests occasionally conflict, and one has to take precedence. Parents certainly have a right to know what their teenager is up to, but that right pales in comparison with the public health interest in eliminating the spread of sexually transmitted diseases.

From an adolescent-psychology point of view, confidentiality is absolutely essential. It is uppermost in the minds of many teenagers coming to a clinic or doctor's office—even if they are only coming to have a sore throat looked at. But this doesn't automatically mean that parents are completely shut out of their teenagers' lives. For one thing, physicians will *always* try to get teenagers either to talk to their parents or to allow the physician to talk to them. We understand that these are important health matters and that usually your teenager will benefit if you know about the situation. But if they say "No way," then we have to respect that. Second, there are times when we will breach a teenager's right to confidentiality. We have to, by law, when we see a suicidal or homicidal adolescent. In those situations, your right to know exceeds the teenager's right to confidentiality. And the overriding public health interest is on your side as well. Third, you should feel confident in knowing that your physician is acting as a parent surrogate. If a teenager comes to see us and asks for birth control, we do not open the cupboard, hand her a package of pills, and wish her good luck and Godspeed. We talk to her, we screen her for STDs, we try to determine what high-risk behaviors, if any, she is engaging in. Occasionally we see a young teenage girl who is being pressured into having sex by her boyfriend, and we support her right to say no. In other words, we're on *your* side! We want the best for your child. We tend toward being a little maternalistic or paternalistic anyway, or we wouldn't have gone into primary-care medicine, and many of us have children of our own. We treat your teenagers the way we would want our teenagers treated.

Obviously, it is far easier if parents are aware of this issue of confidentiality ahead of time. Dr. Hy Tolmas, a good friend of mine and an outstanding physician who has been in private practice in Metairie, Louisiana, for more than thirty years, sends the following letter to his patients' parents when the youngster reaches age eleven:

Dear Mr. and Mrs. Jones:

Now that Amy is eleven years old and has entered adolescence, there are some things I would like to bring to your attention that are important to ensure the positive continuity of care.

As you are aware, in addition to the physical and sexual changes that are taking place, there are significant changes in attitudes and feelings at this age.

On future visits to the office, I will address Amy relative to her reason(s) for the visit, and I will explain the treatment plan to her. It is most important that she understand that I regard her as my patient and respect her feelings, wishes, and concerns. As an integral part of this new relationship, we must all be cognizant of the confidential nature of our interactions. There will be some things that Amy will feel comfortable talking about only to me. I very much appreciate your understanding the effectiveness of this new adolescent/doctor relationship, and I think that Amy will appreciate it as well.

Another goal of this special relationship is to make Amy aware of the importance of her own role in accepting some of the responsibility for her health care. If there are some questions or problems you would like to discuss, I will be delighted to meet with you.

I enjoy treating your children and look forward to many more years of continuing medical care. It is important that we make your adolescent feel at ease. I know we will all continue to be proud of our budding young adult as we watch her grow.

The point of all this is to reassure you that if you can find a physician with whom you and your teenager are

both comfortable—and you use that person appropriately
—you will be making one of the most significant contributions to your teenager's (and your own) health and welfare that you can make. It's like having a backup parent
who, like you, is trying as hard as he can to make sure
that no harm comes to your son or daughter. This also
means that your teenager should have an annual exam.
Unfortunately, most insurance companies will not pay for
this; nor is this yet the official policy of organizations like
the American Academy of Pediatrics. But it should be, and
eventually it will be. Taking your teenager to see the doctor only every two or three years is a prescription for disaster. So much can happen between the ages of twelve
and fifteen, or fifteen and eighteen, that even if your insurance company or health maintenance organization
(HMO) does not cover annual exams, you should consider
paying for them yourself. Think of it as an additional insurance policy, and the cost is probably well under a
hundred dollars a year. Relying on a sports physical or
a camp physical to pick up these sorts of problems is
not sufficient. Often, these physical exams are done in an
assembly-line fashion, by medical personnel who don't
know your teenager and are screening for disqualifying
problems; and privacy (and, therefore, confidentiality) is
impossible.

Your teenager's physician will be able to detect problems long before you will be, although she will need your
help to do so. Monica and Benny might have been diagnosed (and therefore begun treatment) months earlier, if
their parents had brought them in for a checkup. Many
parents I have talked to are afraid that their teenagers will
not come in to see a doctor. But I have yet to hear about a
teenager who refused "a routine checkup, just to make
sure you're healthy and okay." If anything, teenagers are

more concerned about their bodies than you are, and they welcome the chance to talk with a sympathetic and knowledgeable health professional. Of course, if your pediatrician or family physician does not fit this description, then you may indeed have a problem.

What is an adolescent medicine specialist? Adolescent medicine is a field that has existed only since the mid-1950s and didn't really get into high gear until the 1970s. Most of us are pediatricians, although a few are either family practitioners or internists. We have all completed our primary-care training, which for pediatrics involves three years of internship and residency after finishing medical school; and then we have done an additional one to three years of work exclusively with teenagers. This latter period is called fellowship training. After fellowship, adolescent medicine specialists can choose a variety of career options: primary practice in pediatrics, primary practice in adolescent medicine, academic medicine, etc. At the moment, there are approximately a thousand of us in the United States. Many of us are delighted to see your teenager and become his primary physician, but I think that most of us would like to teach the new generation of interns and residents in pediatrics and family practice how to take care of teenagers so that, ideally, you wouldn't have to switch doctors when your child reached puberty. We also serve as a resource for primary-care physicians in our areas, so that we frequently answer questions by phone and see patients in consultation. Many specialists also work in clinics, some of them located in high schools, which brings us to the controversy surrounding school-based health clinics (SBHCs).

SBHCs developed because teenagers were turned off by the traditional health care system and not getting the medical attention they needed. The reasoning was very simple: If teenagers won't come to see us, we'll go to see them. There are a variety of reasons why teenagers are reluctant to go see their family doctor or go to a clinic: worries about confidentiality, having to wait a long time, having to wait in the same room with babies or old people, unsympathetic doctors or nurses, lack of transportation, lack of money or medical coverage, etc. The SBHC movement developed to alleviate many of these problems and concerns. For some reason—probably the squeamishness of the "moral minority"—these clinics were immediately categorized as birth control clinics. This is a serious distortion of what SBHCs are, why they originated, and what they do. In every study that has examined why teenagers use SBHCs—and in most schools the majority of the students do use them—only 10 to 30 percent of the visits are for family planning issues. The vast majority of visits are for acute illnesses, immunizations, acne, sports injuries, drug-use prevention, and counseling. Of the more than three hundred SBHCs in the United States, only a handful actually dispense contraceptives. Certainly none of them is equipped for or involved in doing abortions, which is a frequent accusation, designed to confuse the issue. The clinics do identify teenagers who are sexually active, and therefore at risk of pregnancy or STDs, but such teenagers *need* to be identified, for their own good and society's best interests as well. Traditionally, adolescents have been one of the most medically underserved populations in the United States, and SBHCs go a long way toward trying to change this unfortunate situation. If your teenager's high school or middle school has a clinic, be thankful. If it doesn't, think about trying to give some support to the principal, or local physicians in your area, who might be interested in starting one.

SBHCs and your pediatrician or family physician are key elements in identifying teenagers at risk; and, as I have tried to demonstrate throughout the earlier chapters, nearly all teenagers at some point engage in some activity that puts them at risk. So the short answer to the first question implicit in this chapter's title is: You *always* need to worry! This is not news to you, because, being a parent, you probably do anyway. But you can worry less if you have good medical services on your side—services that will help to screen your teenagers for the very things that can cause them irreparable harm: sexual activity; the use of alcohol, cigarettes, and other drugs; eating disorders; depression.

In general, most parents are well attuned to their teenagers' health, moods, and state of mind. But occasionally it might be useful to think of their lives in terms of the five boxes pictured below:

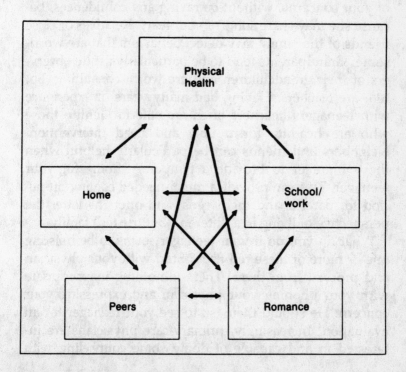

All the boxes are interrelated. Assuming the teenager is ordinarily healthy and well-adjusted, new situations that should cause parents particular concern include:

- A falloff in school performance
- An abrupt change of friends
- The breakup of a long-term relationship
- A sudden uninterest in a previous major hobby or sport
- A dramatic change in mood, energy level, or activity level
- A change in eating or sleeping patterns

Outside verification may be useful as well. For example, your teenager's best friend may be able to validate some of your concerns, without betraying any confidences, because she may share some of your fears. Relatives or close friends of the family may detect behaviors that are worrisome. Grandparents tend to be particularly astute observers of their grandchildren and are worth consulting. So, too, are teachers. Having had many years of experience with teenagers, teachers often are able to identify those who are heading for trouble and need intervention. Neighbors and friends can be particularly helpful when they volunteer to provide a temporary home for your teenager. This can provide a much-needed cooling-off period for parents and their teens, and offer the latter the perspective of living in a different (but trusted) family.

What do you do if your teenager seems to be hoisting one or more of these red flags? Start with your physician and proceed from there. There is nothing inappropriate with your phoning your physician and expressing your concern. He should then ask to see your teenager for an evaluation. Increasingly, primary-care physicians are interested in and capable of doing some counseling with families, if that is what is needed. Since your teenager presumably knows and trusts the physician already, sometimes this is far easier than hauling her off to see a psychologist or psychiatrist. Primary physicians can do well with teenagers who have minor adjustment problems or families that are having a difficult time coping with their teenager's normal adolescence. But sometimes a consultation or referral to a mental health professional is necessary, especially in cases of attempted suicide, moderate or severe depression, psychosis, heavy involvement in drugs, or eating disorders. At times your primary-care physician may even want to accompany you on the first visit, to ease the transition, or to serve as cotherapist with the psychologist or psychiatrist.

How do you know which psychologist or psychiatrist to see? Here again, your teenager's doctor should be very familiar with who works well with teenage patients. The mental health professional's credentials—Ph.D., M.D., M.S.W.—matter far less than her interest in and skill with teenagers. The same is true of whether she trained at Harvard, Yale, or the University of New Mexico. She could have trained at one of the former institutions and been ranked at the absolute bottom of her class, or trained at a state institution because of financial considerations and been considered absolutely brilliant. The one exception to this is that if your teenager requires medication of any sort, a psychiatrist will have to be involved, since an M.D. degree is necessary to prescribe medications.

Similarly, whether a teenager requires inpatient or outpatient treatment will depend upon the judgment of the consultant or specialist involved, in conjunction with your primary physician. Unfortunately, in the 1990s one's choice and type of medical insurance seems to determine a large part of this as well, but certain situations require at least a brief hospitalization: a suicide attempt of any kind or any severity; anorexia nervosa with severe weight loss or refractory to outpatient treatment; and severe drug abuse. Monica, for example, was initially treated as an outpatient by me and an excellent child psychiatrist, but when she continued to lose weight she required hospitalization at an adolescent medicine unit. Benny required hospitalization immediately, both for his psychiatric problems and to shield him from further drug involvement.

Finally, let's talk about the worst-case scenarios. For example, your son is not only using drugs but selling them. Your daughter is using cocaine and having sex with a man twice her age. And neither will listen to you or your spouse—*at all*. They will not accompany you to see the doctor, they will not observe your house rules, and they just come and go as they please. In other words, what if anything can we do about the out-of-control teenager?

Let me make something clear from the beginning: We are talking here about very few teenagers, and many of these scenarios can be avoided if the teenagers can be identified at an early stage of their disorder. Also, frequently these are teenagers who come from chaotic or disorganized families, with serious pathology of their own. The likelihood that you and your spouse, with an intact family and a conscientious approach to child rearing, will have to face this sort of predicament is fortunately very low.

The ancient medical dictum "extreme diseases require desperate remedies" becomes applicable here. These are teenagers who have now passed beyond the usual barrier of parental authority. What's going to stop them? Often the answer is, the law. The next level of authority in our society, after parents, is the judge. Despite the many imperfections of the juvenile justice system in the United States, occasionally a judge will be able to do what parents cannot do—exert some control over a teenager. In very extreme situations, parents have even filed to have their parental obligations terminated—emancipation in reverse —through a Child In Need of Supervision (CHINS) petition from the county court. In such cases, the teenager is completely out of control, the parents have exhausted all possible remedies, and they fear the legal and financial repercussions of their teenager's continued illegal activities.

The only other firm boundaries in such situations are the walls of a secure (locked) inpatient adolescent treatment unit. For severe drug involvement, such units are mandatory. A locked unit is the only way to ensure that a teenager will stay clean while undergoing treatment and rehabilitation. Likewise, such a unit will prevent severely disturbed teenagers harming themselves or others. But with severely rebellious adolescents, parents and physicians must carefully weigh the risks and benefits of confining teenagers against their will.

Chapter 8

Summing Up

❏

To let go when we want to hold on requires utmost gener-
osity and love. Only parents are capable of such painful
greatness.

—Haim Ginott,
Between Parent & Teenager

Some things never change. Parenting has always been a
tough job—one of the toughest. But it is also one of the
most rewarding. The joy of watching children grow and
develop—particularly our own children, with our own
guidance—can not be equaled.

On the other hand, some things do change: the complexity of American society, new and more dangerous
drugs, attitudes about sex and sexuality, new viruses like
HIV and new diseases like AIDS, and the power of the
now ubiquitous media to influence our lives. We are living
in the best of times and the worst of times.

Given these changes, adolescence has become a genu-
inely risky business. But we, as parents, can help to min-

imize some of those risks—through our own education
efforts, by knowing how to communicate effectively with
our kids, and by starting the process early, during their
childhood. We also have to develop some media savvy of
our own and try to make the media work for us rather
than against us. We need to realize that we have important allies who can help us to be better parents and relieve
some of the stresses that inevitably accompany parenting:
physicians, teachers, relatives and friends. The book-
shelves also have never contained so many volumes on
parenting and child rearing.

We are children of the fifties and sixties. Ours was perhaps the most idealistic generation in the history of the
United States. Certainly it was the most contentious. But
what exactly did we accomplish? Have we succeeded in
making the world a better place to live? We were instru-
mental in catalyzing public opinion against the Vietnam
War, but that war has been replaced by other wars. Even
some of the radicals of the sixties have taken the money
and run. American politics has changed dramatically from
the days of the elegantly intellectual Adlai Stevenson and
the idealistic Gene McCarthy to the scandals of the Nixon
and Reagan years. Reagan's place in history is still being
decided, but consider this: We will be paying off his debts
—the national deficit—for the next two generations; we
never had a "homeless problem" until his presidency; and
his Supreme Court appointments will ensure that we will
be subjected to the Reagan philosophy for decades to
come. Meanwhile, while we were growing up, the adults
around us were creating their own Frankenstein monster
—the media. They, too, have gotten out of control. As a
New York Times commentator recently wrote:

Irrelevant.
The label has been slapped on television periodically

over the decades, but now it threatens to become permanent as the industry, led by the commercial networks, brazenly denies even the slightest pretense it might have had to social and cultural responsibility.

. . . Television is no ordinary business. Its very prevalence in the lives of most citizens makes the medium the dominant force in conveying attitudes and values for the whole of society. Anyone who has ever watched television with a child knows first-hand how frighteningly influential the small screen can be in suggesting not only what to buy but also how to behave and speak and, indeed, what to think.

On this level alone, television's responsibility is staggering. But these days too many television executives seemed determined to evade that point as they prattle on about programming that is simply considered "product," as innocuous as another brand of soap.

> —John J. O'Connor,
> *The New York Times*,
> June 9, 1991

In short, we failed. We may have had fun at times, but we failed.

But, as in a good Hollywood movie, we're down but not out, wounded but not fatally. We've got one more good run left in us. And that run is our children. We may not have been successful in changing the world, but perhaps we aimed for too much. We need to start smaller—with our kids. If we teach them the principles that we were once so enamored of—world peace, nonviolence, civil rights, equal rights, and respect for the environment—perhaps we can still achieve our goal, just not in our own lifetimes. So here's to growing up in the sixties, and to modern parenting in the nineties. I hope—as Crosby, Stills, Nash and Young once sang—that you will "teach your children well."

Appendix I

Recommended Readings
and Films

❏

GENERAL ADOLESCENCE AND PARENTING OF ADOLESCENTS

Ames, Louise B., and Frances L. Ilg. *Your Ten to Fourteen Year Old*. New York: Delacorte Press, 1988.

Bettelheim, Bruno. *A Good Enough Parent*. New York: Vintage Books, 1987.

Blume, Judy. *Letters to Judy: What Your Kids Wish They Could Tell You*. New York: Putnam's, 1986.

Elkind, David. *A Sympathetic Understanding of the Child, Birth to Sixteen*. Boston: Allyn & Bacon, 1978.

————. *All Grown Up and No Place to Go: Teenagers in Crisis*. Reading, Mass.: Addison-Wesley, 1984.

————. *The Hurried Child: Growing Up Too Fast Too Soon*. Reading, Mass.: Addison-Wesley, 1989.

Fleming, Don. *How to Stop the Battle with Your Teenager*. New York: Prentice Hall Press, 1989.

Gilligan, Carol. *Making Connections: Relational Worlds of Adolescent Girls at Emma Willard School*. New York: Harvard University Press, 1990.

Ginott, Hain G. *Between Parent & Teenager*. New York: Avon, 1971.

Gore, Tipper. *Raising PG Kids in an X-Rated Society*. New York: Bantam, 1989.

Greydanus, Donald E., ed. *The American Academy of Pediatrics' Adolescent Book*. New York: Bantam, 1991.

Lickona, Thomas. *Raising Good Children: From Birth Through the Teenage Years*. New York: Bantam, 1985.

Patterson, Gerald, and Marion Forgatch. *Parents and Adolescents: Living Together. I. The Basics. II. Family Problem Solving*. Eugene, Oreg.: Castalia Publishing Co., 1987.

Powell, Douglas H. *Teenagers: When to Worry and What to Do*. New York: Doubleday, 1986.

Rinzler, Carol E. *Your Adolescent: An Owner's Manual*. New York: Atheneum, 1981.

Rosemond, John. *Six-Point Plan for Raising Happy, Healthy Children*. Kansas City: Andrews and McMeel, 1989.

Simons, Janet M., Belva Finlay, and Alice Yang. *The Adolescent & Young Adult Fact Book*. Washington, D.C.: Children's Defense Fund, 1991.

Steinberg, Laurence, and Ann Levine. *You & Your Adolescent: A Parent's Guide for Ages 10–20*. New York: Harper & Row, 1990.

Winn, Marie. *Children Without Childhood*. New York: Penguin, 1984.

Winship, Elizabeth C. *Reaching Your Teenager*. Boston: Houghton Mifflin, 1982.

SEX AND SEXUALITY

For Children

Andry, Andrew, and Steven Schepp. *How Babies Are Made*. Boston: Little, Brown, 1984.

Gordon, Sol, and Judith Gordon. *Did the Sun Shine Before You Were Born?* Syracuse: Ed-U-Press, 1982.

Mayle, Peter. *Where Did I Come From?* New Jersey: Lyle Stuart, 1973.

Ratner, Marilyn, and Susan Chamlin. *Straight Talk: Sexuality Education for Parents and Kids 4–7*. New York: Viking Penguin, 1987.

For Teenagers and Preteens

Bell, Ruth. *Changing Bodies, Changing Lives: A Book for Teens on Sex and Relationships.* New York: Vintage Books, 1988.

Boston Women's Health Book Collective. *The New Our Bodies, Ourselves.* Revised and Updated for the Nineties. New York: Simon & Schuster, 1992.

Gordon, Sol. *Seduction Lines Heard 'Round the World and Answers You Can Give.* Fayetteville, N.Y.: Ed-U-Press, 1987.

———. *Why Love Is Not Enough.* Holbrook, Mass.: Bob Adams, 1990.

Hein, Karen, and Theresa Digeronimo. *AIDS: Trading Fears for Facts.* New York: Consumer Reports Books, 1989.

Johnson, Eric W. *People, Love, Sex, and Families: Answers to Questions Preteens Ask.* New York: Walker, 1985.

Madaras, Lynda. *What's Happening to My Body Book for Boys.* New York: Newmarket Press, 1988.

———. *What's Happening to My Body Book for Girls.* New York: Newmarket Press, 1988.

Masland, Robert P., Jr. *What Teenagers Want to Know about Sex.* Boston: Little, Brown, 1988.

Mayle, Peter. *What's Happening to Me?* New Jersey: Lyle Stuart, 1975.

McCoy, Kathy, and Charles Wibbelsman. *Growing and Changing: A Handbook for Preteens.* New York: Putnam, 1986.

———. *The New Teenage Body Book.* Los Angeles: The Body Press, 1987.

Miller, Deborah A., and Alex Waigandt. *Coping with Your Sexual Orientation: A Review.* New York: Rosen Publishing Group, 1990.

Planned Parenthood Federation of America. *That Growing Feeling: Facts of Life for Teens and Preteens.* New York: Planned Parenthood Federation of America, 1984.

Westheimer, Ruth, and Nathan Kravetz. *First Love: A Young People's Guide to Sexual Information.* New York: Warner Books, 1985.

For Parents

American Academy of Pediatrics Committee on Adolescence. *Sex Education: A Bibliography of Educational Materials for Children, Adolescents, and Their Families*. Elk Grove Village, Ill.: American Academy of Pediatrics, 1988.

Bell, Ruth. *Changing Bodies, Changing Lives*. New York: Random House, 1988.

Calderone, Mary S., and James W. Ramey. *Talking with Your Child about Sex*. New York: Ballantine, 1982.

Cassell, Carol. *Straight from the Heart: How to Talk to Your Teenagers About Love and Sex*. New York: Simon & Schuster, 1987.

Fairchild, Betty. *Now That You Know: What Every Parent Should Know About Homosexuality*. San Diego: Harcourt Brace Jovanovich, 1989.

Gordon, Sol, and Judith Gordon. *Raising a Child Conservatively in a Sexually Permissive World*. New York: Simon & Schuster, 1989.

Gordon, Sol, and C. W. Snyder. *Personal Issues in Human Sexuality: A Guidebook for Better Sexual Health*, 2d edition. Boston: Allyn and Bacon, 1989.

Alan Guttmacher Institute. *Risk and Responsibility: Teaching Sex Education in America's Schools Today*. New York: Alan Guttmacher Institute, 1989.

Masland, Robert P., Jr. *What Teenagers Want to Know about Sex*. Boston: Little, Brown, 1988.

Wattleton, Faye, and staff. *How to Talk with Your Child About Sexuality*. New York: Doubleday, 1986.

Weisman, Betty, and Michael Weisman. *What We Told Our Kids About Sex*. San Diego: Harcourt Brace Jovanovich, 1987.

Winship, Elizabeth C. *Reaching your Teenager*. Boston: Houghton Mifflin, 1982.

MISCELLANEOUS

For Teenagers

Gordon, Sol. *When Living Hurts*. New York: Union of American Hebrew Congregations, 1985.

Leder, Jane M. *Dead Serious: A Book for Teenagers About Teen Suicide*. New York: Atheneum, 1987.

McCoy, Kathy. *The Teenage Survival Guide*. New York: Simon & Schuster, 1981.

For Parents

Berman, Claire. *Making It as a Stepparent: New Roles/New Rules*. New York: Harper & Row, 1986.

Dodson, Fitzhugh. *How to Single Parent*. New York: Harper & Row, 1987.

Dupont, Robert L. *Getting Tough on Gateway Drugs: A Guide for the Family*. Washington, D.C.: American Psychiatric Press, 1984.

Forrest, Gary G. *How to Cope with a Teenage Drinker: New Alternatives and Hope for Parents*. New York: Atheneum, 1983.

Gardner, Richard A. *The Parents' Book About Divorce*. New York: Bantam, 1982.

Hahn, Julie. *"Have You Done Your Homework?": A Parent's Guide to Helping Teenagers Succeed in School*. New York: Wiley, 1985.

Mack, John, and Holly Hickler. *Vivienne, the Life and Suicide of an Adolescent Girl*. Boston: Little, Brown, 1981.

McCoy, Kathy. *Coping with Teenage Depression*. New York: Signet Press, 1982.

Polson, Beth, and Miller Newton. *Not My Kid: A Parent's Guide to Kids and Drugs*. New York: Avon, 1985.

Wallerstein, Judith S., and Joan B. Kelly. *Surviving the Breakup: How Children and Parents Cope with Divorce*. New York: Basic Books, 1980.

TEN RECOMMENDED BOOKS ABOUT ADOLESCENTS

The Diary of Anne Frank (Anne Frank)
A Separate Peace (John Knowles)
The Catcher in the Rye (J. D. Salinger)
Ordinary People (Judith Guest)
Endless Love (Scott Spenser)
Rounding Third & Heading Home (Victor Strasburger)

The Secret Diary of Adrian Mole, Aged 13¾ (Sue Townsend)
The Growing Pains of Adrian Mole (Sue Townsend)
The Outsiders (S. E. Hinton)
The Chosen (Chaim Potok)

MEDIA

Books and Monographs:

Center for Population Options. *Talking with TV: A Guide for Grown-Ups and Kids*. Washington, D.C.: CPO, 1991.

Dietz, William H., Victor Strasburger. "Television, Children, and Adolescents." *Current Problems in Pediatrics*, Vol. 21, January 1991.

Gore, Tipper. *Raising PG Kids in an X-Rated Society*. New York: Bantam, 1989.

Jurs, Addie. *TV—Becoming Unglued: A Guide to Improve Children's TV Habits*. San Marcos, CA: Robert Erdmann Publishing, 1992.

Keeshan, Bob. *Growing Up Happy*. New York: Berkley Books, 1991.

Liebert, Robert M., and Joyce Sprafkin. *The Early Window—Effects of Television on Children and Youth*, 3d edition. New York: Pergamon Press, 1988.

Palmer, Edward L. *Television and America's Children: A Crisis of Neglect*. New York: Oxford University Press, 1988.

Singer, Dorothy G., Jerome L. Singer, and Diana M. Zuckerman. *Use TV to Your Child's Advantage*. Reston, VA: Acropolis Books, 1990.

Winn, Marie. *Children without Childhood*. New York: Penguin, 1984.

———. *The Plug-In Drug*. New York: Viking, 1985.

Curricula

The Degrassi Health Education Curriculum: This is a six-part curriculum, based on the popular TV series *Degrassi Junior High* and *Degrassi High*, that deals with such major adolescent health issues a relationships, teen pregnancy, HIV/AIDS, date abuse, sexual orientation, and alcoholism. Included in the units are background information, the video, discussion questions, group activities, parent/adult interviews, reproducible student handouts, and additional resources. The six videos are available at $50/video from: Direct Cinema, P.O. Box 69799, Los Angeles, CA 90069-9976 (phone: 800-525-0000).

The Degrassi Health Education Curriculum can be used with or without the videotapes and is available for $5 postage and handling from: WGBH, Health Curriculum, Box 2222, South Easton, MA 02375.

Implementing the Children's Television Act: Action for Children's Television: *Choices for Children: An Action Kit to Implement the Children's Television Act.* Cambridge, Mass.: Action for Children's Television, 1991.

Teaching Media Literacy: *Parenting in a TV Age—A Media Literacy Workshop Kit on Children and Television.* Available for $21.95 from Center for Media and Values, 1962 South Shenandoah Street, Los Angeles, CA 90034 (phone: 301-559-2944).

TWENTY-FIVE RECOMMENDED FILMS ABOUT CHILDHOOD AND ADOLESCENCE

Anne of Green Gables
Boyz 'n the Hood
Breaking Away
The Flamingo Kid
Harold and Maude
Heathers
Hope & Glory
Karate Kid
Little Mermaid
Lucas
Metropolitan
My American Cousin
My Bodyguard

My Father's Glory
My Life as a Dog
My Mother's Castle
Ordinary People
Pump Up the Volume
Ramblin' Rose
Au Revoir les Enfants
Say Anything
A Separate Peace
Streetwise
Sugar Cane Alley
The Sure Thing

Organizations to Contact for Further Information

❑

American Academy of
  Pediatrics
141 Northwest Point
  Boulevard
P.O. Box 927
Elk Grove Village, IL 60009
(800) 433-9016

Center for Population
  Options
1025 Vermont Avenue,
  N.W.
Suite 210
Washington, DC 20005
(202) 347-5700

Children's Defense Fund
25 E Street, N.W.
Washington, DC 20001
(202) 628-8787

National Federation of
  Parents & Friends of
  Lesbians & Gays, Inc.
  (P-FLAG)
1012 Fourteenth Street,
  N.W., 6th Floor
Washington, DC 20005
(202) 638-3852

National Gay & Lesbian
  Task Force
1734 Fourteenth Street,
  N.W.
Washington, D.C. 20009-
  4309
(202) 332-6483
(800) 221-7044

Planned Parenthood
  Federation of America
810 Seventh Avenue
New York, NY 10019
(212) 541-7800

Sexual Information and
  Educational Council of the
  U.S. (SIECUS)
80 Fifth Avenue, Suite 801
New York, NY 10011
(212) 819-9770

Society for Adolescent
  Medicine
19401 E. Highway 40
Independence, MO 64055
(816) 795-8336

NETWORKS

ABC
Entertainment President
2040 Avenue of the Stars, 5th
  Floor
Los Angeles, CA 90067

CBS
Entertainment President
7800 Beverly Boulevard
Los Angeles, CA 90036

NBC
Entertainment President
3000 West Alameda
Burbank, CA 91523

Fox Broadcasting
President
P.O. Box 900
Los Angeles, CA 90213

ACTIVIST GROUP

American Academy of Pediatrics
Committee on Communications
141 Northwest Point Boulevard
P.O. Box 927
Elk Grove Village, IL 60009-0927

FEDERAL COMMUNICATIONS COMMISSION

Mass Media Bureau
Enforcement Division, Room 8210
2025 M Street, N.W.
Washington, DC 20554

Index

❑

About the Author

❑

Victor Strasburger, M.D., is Chief of the Division of Adolescent Medicine and Associate Professor of Pediatrics at the University of New Mexico School of Medicine in Albuquerque. He is a national consultant to the National PTA and is a member of the American Academy of Pediatrics' subcommittee on Television and Children. A graduate of Yale College and Harvard Medical School, he did a pediatric internship and residency at Children's Hospital in Seattle, followed by a senior residency and fellowship at Children's Hospital in Boston. He also directed the Adolescent Medicine Training Program at Bridgeport Hospital in Connecticut, where he was an Associate Clinical Professor of Pediatrics at Yale Medical School.